W9-AGE-577

CONNECT!

HOW TO GET YOUR KIDS TO TALK TO YOU

CARL B. SMITH, PH.D.

WITH

SUSAN MOKE AND MARJORIE R. SIMIC

College Park Elementary
2811 Barnard Street
Indianapolis, IN 46268

Family Literacy Center

EDINFO
PRESS

Published 1994 by the Family Literacy Center, Indiana University, 2805 East Tenth Street, Suite 150, Bloomington, Indiana 47408-2698, and EDINFO Press, P.O. Box 5953, Bloomington, IN 47407

Design/Production: Lauren Bongiani Gottlieb
Cover: David J. Smith
Illustrations: Tyagan Miller

Copyright © 1994 by Carl B. Smith. All rights reserved.

This publication results from the *Parents Sharing Books* project which was developed and evaluated with support from the Lilly Endowment, Inc. Participants have been encouraged to express freely their judgments in matters regarding this project. Points of view or opinions, however, do not necessarily represent the official view or opinions of either the Lilly Endowment, Inc. or Indiana University.

Library of Congress Cataloging-in-Publication Data

Smith, Carl Bernard.
    Connect! : how to get your kids to talk to you / Carl B. Smith
with Susan Moke and Marjorie R. Simic.
      p. cm.
    Includes bibliographical references and index.
    ISBN 0-927516-43-8 : $14.95
    1. Reading--Parent participation. 2. Parenting. 3. Parent and
child. 4. Communication in the family. I. Moke, Susan, 1949-
II. Simic, Marjorie R. (Marjorie Rose), 1951- . III. Title. IV. Title:
How to get your kids to talk to you.
LB1050.2.S65   1994
649'.58--dc20   93-29336
                                            CIP

TABLE OF CONTENTS

Table of Contents (continued)

Table of Contents (continued)

Table of Contents (continued)

DEDICATION

To my son, Tony, who started me thinking about family communication through books
and who challenged me constantly to respect
his ideas.

— With Love

ACKNOWLEDGEMENTS

The experiences that preceded this book and provided its substance were coordinated by a marvelous group of people in the Family Literacy Center at Indiana University. We all had the good fortune to work on a project known as *Parents Sharing Books*. Without these people the material for this book would have lain hidden. How lucky I am to have them as co-workers.

Michael Shermis organized events and budgets with high energy and enthusiasm as the project manager. Melinda Hamilton answered questions and wrote book reviews for the hundreds of project participants. Ellie Macfarlane helped conduct our numerous leader training workshops. Marge Simic gathered the evaluation data and helped select the parent and child quotes used in this book. She also used her considerable experience in guiding the development of our leader training manual. Susan Moke acted as our wordsmith and exercised her deft editorial hand in our many publications, especially in this book. Eugene Reade added his usual careful proofreading touch to this manuscript.

It is not my intention to make these people responsible for any of the ideas or opinions expressed in this book. I take full charge of them, but want all to know that I am in great debt and offer my thanks to these lovely people for assisting me in bringing this book to print.

CBS
Bloomington, Indiana
September, 1993

CONNECT! HOW TO GET YOUR KIDS TO TALK TO YOU

This is a book with a story to tell. The stories you will hear as you read the book have one thing in common: they all acknowledge the problems with and need for family communication.

Psychologists, marriage counselors, and our own intuition remind us that healthy communication reduces our feelings of isolation and helps us guide our children through school and toward independent adulthood. But how do we accomplish this? This book describes the success stories of parents and children who learned to talk to each other by following a simple, straightforward program. Each chapter explains a step in that program and gives the stories of parents and children who succeeded in that step. My own story gives us a place to start.

When my son was thirteen, he came home with a science fiction book one of his teachers suggested that he might enjoy reading. My son loved science, but he hated to read. I think this clever teacher was trying to use his interest in science to lure him into reading. She had suggested the book *Dune* by Frank Herbert.

"Hey Dad," he said, "this book is about people who live on a desert planet. You know, no rain. How do you think they can survive?"

By a miracle, I thought—just like this miracle that has my son reading a big, hefty book. But I replied, "What an interesting challenge. How would you and I survive on a planet like that?"

"I don't know," he said. "I've only read a few pages. The back cover says that water is only one of their problems. Huge predators called 'sand worms' swim through the desert sand looking for people to snack on. Yum!"

"Wow!" I exclaimed. "Can I read the first chapter when you're finished?"

And so began the great adventure of a thirteen-year-old reluctant reader and his dad. Chapter by chapter we read about warring groups who fought to control the forbidding planet, Dune. Day by day, we retold and analyzed what we had read and tried to predict what would happen next. We checked out the science (mostly biology and some astronomy) that made it possible for human beings to live in an atmosphere where it no longer rained. We winked knowingly at each other over their love affairs, and staged mock battles on my son's bed to see if we would have used different tactics from those the Duke of Dune used to ward off his invaders. The setting was perfect—my son's room often resembled a war zone.

That was the beginning of a fresh chapter in our lives. With our shared reading of *Dune*, my son began to read more. More importantly, he and I began to talk more. Focusing on the *Dune* adventure gave us something besides our family relationship to discuss. Now I had something to say to him besides "Clean your room!" or "Be home by 9:00 or else!" And he didn't feel obligated to fight me for his independence. Instead, we were fighting pirate invaders together. We were speculating about the stirrings of young love. We were having a good time reading the same book. Our relationship changed significantly.

My son didn't become an avid reader, but he began to read more regularly, and we regularly shared a book. That's the simple program I mentioned—increasing family reading and thereby improving family communication. With my son, I had the advantage of being a teacher trained in how to discuss books with kids. Now, after working with hundreds of families in our *Parents Sharing Books* program, I am convinced that all parents can share books with their kids if they have a little guidance.

As you read this book, you will hear the voices of many parents and children telling their own stories. Their stories have something in common with the one I have just shared with you. Each of them shows how family book sharing has helped parents and their children connect with each other in new and satisfying ways. One parent says "this program really bridged the gap between my child and me." Another mother tells us that family book sharing taught her and her child how to relate to one another in a more meaningful way. She says "the project was especially on time for us. Communication was at an all-time low, and this project certainly helped open up our line of communication with each other."

These parents are talking about a program called *Parents Sharing Books*. It's an idea developed through the Family Literacy Center at Indiana University, Bloomington, and partially funded by the Lilly Endowment. The Family Literacy Center has shown hundreds of parents and children how reading and sharing selected books can make a difference in their family relationships.

The *Parents Sharing Books* program began in dozens of middle schools. We wanted to test the program's power with parents and children who were at what is typically the most difficult stage in their relationship: the preteen years when children often stand up and yell, "I'm out of here," and begin to drift away from their parents. We worked through schools in order to reach parents and kids, but the ideas do not rely on teachers' professional expertise or on the school curriculum for success. Nonetheless, many teachers have taken leadership roles in setting up family book-sharing programs because they have discovered that children's school work improves and that class discussions about books take on a dynamic character when parents and kids read and share together.

The Family Literacy Center at Indiana University conducts training programs for parents and teachers who want to lead groups of parents and children in book-sharing activities. Those training seminars prepare leaders to organize family book clubs as self-help groups of parents and children who meet regularly to work through the steps outlined in this book.

What you have in your hand is a "how-to" book. It isn't designed to teach your child to read, but it will show you how to help your child (whether she is three or thirteen) become a better and more enthusiastic reader. This book will help you guide your child toward a first-hand experience of the many pleasures and uses of reading. It will also guide you in your family conversations. The book-sharing strategies you will learn about here are designed to

- strengthen your relationship with your child.
- promote your child's intellectual and emotional growth.
- increase your child's self-esteem.
- improve your child's reading skills and classroom performance.
- help your child appreciate the value of recreational reading.
- enable you to become a more active participant in your child's education.

Each chapter offers down-to-earth advice about how you can enjoy family book sharing at home. Chapter I, *The Many Avenues of Parent/Child Communication*, details ways that family book sharing can allow you and your son or daughter to take a safe step outside of your parent/child roles and meet on neutral ground. This chapter illustrates how the two of you can use conversations about books to share your opinions and values and expectations with one another. One parent evaluates the effect family book sharing has had on her relationship with her child by saying, "This has provided an area of equality for us—we can relate with each other on a little more equal basis. It hasn't been a mother-daughter situation where both of us are trying to win and be right."

Educators' growing insistence that parents need to become actively involved in their children's education comes along when most families must rely on two incomes to sustain their households, and when many homes are single-parent households. Thus, parents find themselves continually pressed for time. Chapter II, *Finding Time—the Old Bugaboo,* addresses this problem by offering practical strategies that will help you make time to participate in your child's education. Most parents and educators agree that strong reading skills are the most reliable predictor of children's educational success. As your child's first and most influential teacher, you can make a difference in your child's classroom performance just by reading and discussing books at home with him on a regular basis. As one parent notes,

> We are busy and it's hard to be a good participant when you are involved in everything...family book sharing is one thing that I felt [my daughter] Leslie thought was really important for us to do. It contributes to our relationship, which is different than most parent councils, school meetings, or advisory boards.

This chapter shows you how you can find time to make book sharing a family habit.

Chapter III, *The Challenge of Motivating Kids,* anticipates problems you may have getting your child interested in sharing ideas with you. This chapter supplies a variety of approaches you can use to set up a plan for family book sharing. Choosing the right books will start you on the right track and it will give your child first-hand experience of the pleasures recreational reading can provide. To that end, Chapter IV, *Guidelines for Selecting Books;* Chapter V, *Books for Ages Three to Nine;* and Chapter VI, *Books for Ages Ten to Fourteen* discuss children's typical reading interests and provide reliable strategies for choosing books you will both enjoy. These chapters also include lists of tried-and-true stories for children of various age groups and reading abilities. You can use the strategies outlined here to select books you and your child will want to read and talk about together.

Chapter VII, *Using Conversations to Share Books,* will give you the nuts-and-bolts of family book sharing. As you read this chapter you will discover how to ask the kinds of questions that will get a discussion going, and you will learn how to respond to your child's statements in a way that encourages— rather than shuts down—conversations once they start. The following chapters (VIII, IX, and X) outline ways you and your child can use writing, art, or drama to share your feelings and ideas. These chapters present a range of approaches specifically designed to engage kids of various ages in conversations about books and reading.

Chapter XI, *Self-Esteem and Reading,* explores the relationship between children's self-image and their reading skills. As you read this chapter you will discover how you can consciously use book-sharing conversations to strengthen your child's self-esteem. In this chapter we rely on research evidence to examine the productive relationship between recreational reading and children's overall educational success.

In the book's final chapter, *Just Do It!,* we briefly list important guidelines for reading and sharing, and we ask you to consider the value of having a mutual support network of parents like yourself who are also interested in making reading a family habit in their homes. These final comments include suggestions about how you can begin a family book club for parents and children in your community.

Many of the chapters in this book end with a short section titled *Bridges to Cross.* At times we all find ourselves making statements that set up barriers instead of building bridges of understanding and cooperation between ourselves and those we care about. For that reason, this section presents negative and positive phrasings of statements parents and children often use to communicate with each other. You will probably recognize some familiar statements in the negative part of this section—I know I did. Don't feel accused. These negative and positive scripts are designed to help you pull down barriers to communication and turn them into bridges.

Because we know parents with children of varying ages and reading abilities will be using this book, we have tried to illustrate how you can use the information and strategies we present here with children of all ages—with toddlers who delight in picture books and with teenagers who love immersing themselves in science fiction or romance novels. If you put these strategies to use in your own home, I am confident that you will discover the many benefits family book sharing can have for you and your children. One fifth-grader has summed up her feelings about sharing books with her mother by saying,

> I think it has brought us closer. Now we can talk about the books we are reading...and I read a lot of them! We ask each other about books and we never did that before. It's just neat to have your mom interested in what you are reading and thinking about, and I like that she is reading things I like to read.

I hope your family book sharing produces results as satisfying as those this youngster describes.

CBS
Bloomington, Indiana

CHAPTER I

THE MANY AVENUES OF PARENT/CHILD COMMUNICATION

I was afraid this idea of reading together and reading the same book would turn my daughter off. But it's been good for both of us. It allowed us to look at each other not as a child and a mother, but people who have opinions, and values, and expectations.

—Barbara Putrich

We actually got a little dialogue going about some feelings. Some ideas came up that I hadn't thought about. My thoughts were completely different from what my son thought.

—Jerry Nugent

Lessons to Live By

Take a moment to stop and consider the conversations you have with your child in a typical day. What do you spend the most time talking to your child about? Most parents spend a lot of time engaging their children in short conversations that begin with questions like "Did you brush your teeth?" "Was it you who forgot to clean up the kitchen after you fixed a snack?" "How can you say that you hate your little brother?"

If each of us spent a day listening to what we say to our children, we would probably discover that most of our interactions with them are directive in nature. We spend a lot of time teaching them how to behave—how to take care of themselves and how to respect the rights and feelings of others. That's okay. After all, that is a parent's role. But unless we periodically have a chance to step outside our directive roles and relate to our children as thinking and feeling individuals, it's hard for us to discover how effective we are. When our children grow into their school years, especially after age seven, we sometimes think more about their school achievement (or sports achievement) than we do about their growth as human beings. We may forget to ask them what they are thinking or what fears and joys they are experiencing. I often wonder why we shift our attention from our concern for their feelings, their sense of self-esteem, and their internal needs to a more judgmental attitude as they grow older. Perhaps we change our perspective when we begin to feel that our children don't need us as much anymore.

The more our children look outside the home and the family for ideas and recreation, the more removed they may seem from us. As they step farther and farther outside the family circle, we parents begin to look at them as "those children over there," instead of as "my children in here." And the more often we look out there to see our children, the less likely we are to bring them in close to ask them what they are thinking and what they are feeling. That's when our communication with our children begins to sound like the barks of an angry drill sergeant. We want them to act politely and to stand as positive symbols of the family because we fear that friends and neighbors will link those children to us, and our children will mar our image if they do not act appropriately.

Generally our children seek independence outside the family—as they should. Unfortunately, as they keep stretching the limits of their family lifeline, we parents often put up own barriers, and thus it becomes increasingly difficult for us to interact with our kids in a personal way. Even our questions at the end of a school day may sound a lot like those of a store clerk checking out school supplies:

"What did you learn in school today?"

"Do you have homework in math?"

"Do you have any papers to show me?"

As a matter of record, those questions are important because they show that the parent values education. I am sure that teachers would rejoice if they thought that all parents were asking those questions at the end of each school day. But questions like that don't create conversations—that is, they don't create the kind of conversations that invite a child to talk about more than just her grade on a test or composition. We need to turn our questions and our conversations to those things that are truly important to our children, to things that invite them to confide their hurts and their joys. For example, an interested parent might ask

"What did you learn today that excited you?

"Were there things that confused you? What can we talk about that might help?"

"Did you read anything today that you would like to share with me? What is it that you like most about this story?"

Lessons to Live By

These questions draw the child into a conversation filled with individual meaning. If a child wants to talk and he sees his parent as a good listener, that parent may receive a frank view of his child at that moment in time. At other times, the same child may walk away from his parent's questions without a word. Especially if a child believes that his parent is prying into matters he doesn't want to share or discuss, he may say nothing, or even express hostility.

Both parents and children sometimes need help figuring out how to communicate about the important things in their lives. Perhaps parent and child have too much baggage standing between them to hold a good conversation, or perhaps there are topics that are too sensitive for them to just throw across the kitchen table. Or perhaps they have conversed so infrequently, they don't quite know how to bring each other into a conversation. It is often much easier for us to talk about someone else's problems than to talk about our own. That's exactly where family book sharing comes into the picture.

Read the Same Book

Have you noticed what happens to conversations when two people have read the same article or the same book? Their interest and energy perk up. They have a bond between them that leads them to describe what they like, to challenge ideas, to wonder aloud what will happen next. They no longer have to rely on shallow chatter-"How are you?" "Fine." "That's good." "Nice day." "Yeah, but it may rain later." They have the common ground of a book they both know and they get excited about exploring that common ground together.

When we talk about a book that we have both read, we can also escape the rigidity of the parent/child roles that often control our thinking. We don't have to represent the authority figure. We can just talk about our perceptions of the actions and ideas in the book. A child can do the same. Listen to Barbara Putrich as she reflects on an early book conversation that she had with her daughter:

> One of the first books we read together was *The Haunting of Francis Rain,* and it was really a fun book for us to share. Some of the discussions Gayle and I had about the books we read surprised me. I thought her opinions were much more adult than I had expected. We talked about the boy-girl relationships in the books and I was surprised at the maturity level at which Gayle approached them. I think both of us learned something about each other that surprised us. Gayle probably expected me to stand up for the parents in these books and frankly, I expected Gayle to stand up for the kid all the time but it wasn't that way. Gayle would talk about the things that the child did wrong and why she thought it was wrong. You hope that you teach your child values and right from wrong, but you're never sure if that's how things will turn out. What these types of conversations have done for me is reassure me that the things we have tried to teach Gayle are part of her and she pulls from that background or upbringing when she talks about these situations in books.

Values to Discuss

Every parent feels the obligation to make sure her child can tell the difference between right and wrong behavior—to teach her child the value of honesty, self-respect, kindness, and hard work. Perhaps you also hold other values in high esteem and are committed to teaching your children how to use those precepts to guide their actions. As a way of bringing this issue into focus for yourself, take a moment to make a short (five or six items) list of the ethics and moral values you want your child to learn to live by.

Values to Guide Life:

1. _____

2. _____

3. _____

4. _____

5. _____

6. _____

After you have made the list, consider how you communicate these values to your child. Many parents see regular church attendance as a way of providing their children with moral lessons to live by. Most of us use family activities and daily chores to teach their children the value of cooperation and hard work. We also teach our ethical and moral standards when we discipline our children and when we help them work through their own personal crises.

For example, one parent reported that her daughter Melinda, age nine, had a friend with whom she had played for months. When the new girl moved into the neighborhood, the previous friend, Tina, seemed to disappear. Then one afternoon when Melinda was on the phone, the parent overheard her saying, "Tina, I have a girl friend. I can have only one special friend, and you're not it." Then Melinda hung up.

"What was that all about?" the mother asked. "Did you and Tina have a fight?"

What she learned was that there was no fight, but the new girl, who was attractive and seemed very self-confident, wanted Melinda as an exclusive friend. Melinda had to ignore or reject other friends if she wanted to keep this new friend.

"Melinda," the mother explained, "you don't need to hurt someone's feelings just because you no longer consider her your best friend. How would you feel if Tina did to you what you just did to her? Besides, what makes you think that you can't have more than one good friend?"

Well, it turned out that Melinda hadn't made that decision on her own. Her new friend had given her an ultimatum: she had to reject Tina or their friendship was finished.

"Melinda," the mother said, "a good friend doesn't ask you to hurt someone else to prove your friendship. More importantly, there is no reason at all that you can't have many good friends. For your sake and for Tina's sake, I want you to call her back to apologize for your unkind words."

Then the mother asked Melinda to set up an after-school work session in their home that would include Tina, the new friend, and at least one or two other classmates. They could work on a school project together and enjoy some refreshments. The mother felt that this kind of gesture would send a message to Melinda's new friend, as well as to Melinda. Shortly after the afternoon work session, the mother noticed that Melinda was on the phone frequently with Tina again, and she was also making plans with other friends. The girl who had insisted on an exclusive relationship chose not to remain in Melinda's circle of friends.

Because Melinda's mother was alert and was willing to take action, she probably minimized the damage that these exclusive relationships can cause for children. Children's books and young adult books recount many variations of Melinda's story: making and losing friends is a part of every child's life. Melinda's mother might have used an incident in a book to help Melinda resolve her friendship problem. As it was, this mother seemed able to handle the problem in a straightforward manner because she respected other people's feelings and wanted her daughter to reflect on the values involved in her actions.

Meeting on Neutral Territory

Engaging in regular book-sharing conversations can be a way of clearing some neutral ground on which you and your kid can meet to discuss things that are important to both of you. It's a way for you to let your child know what you value, what ways of behaving you approve or disapprove of without directing your comments at her and her behavior. We are not suggesting that you use discipline as a primary way of conveying values to children, yet it is one means at your disposal. When you approach a behavior problem with calmness and objectivity, you show your child that her behavior has contradicted a value you want her to learn.

Meeting on Neutral Territory

Family book sharing is a way of starting informal, positive conversations you can use to share your opinions and discuss those values you listed a few pages back. For instance, one father told us a story about reading the picture book *Chrysanthemum*, with his daughter, Melissa. Chrysanthemum, the little mouse who is the book's main character, feels like she has an "absolutely perfect name" until she grows old enough to go to school. On her first day of school, Chrysanthemum's classmates make fun of her because she is named after a flower. Realizing that her name is different from the other children's, Chrysanthemum begins to feel like the name she thought was "absolutely perfect" is, in fact, "absolutely dreadful."

After the father and his daughter had read this story, they began to talk about what it means to be different and not to fit in. That conversation opened the way for Melissa to talk about how "some of the kids at school" made fun of the way a new boy in her class talked (the boy's family had just moved from Mississippi to the small town in Indiana where the girl and her father lived). Melissa admitted that she, too, thought the new boy "was kind of weird." Reading and talking about *Chrysanthemum* gave the father a chance to share his own ideas about what it means to be tolerant of others.

Another parent points out how family book sharing opened new avenues of communication for her and her child:

> I think when we were sharing books, our relationship changed. There was less "telling" in our relationship—less "why didn't you do that?" and less "do this!" There was less abruptness in our conversations and relationship. Taking time for each other gave us time to relate to each other.

Geri Bradford, a mother who now works full-time as a computer service consultant, sees family book sharing as a way to spend some "quality time" with her older daughter and appreciates the way conversations about characters in stories have provided them with an avenue of approach to touchy or controversial issues:

> We have used this time to really talk about things. There may be situations in the book that we are not experiencing, but we still talk about them. I share my beliefs and Leslie knows where I stand on these issues. We can talk about things in a calm manner and I can listen to her talk without anger or fighting. There have been times when having the book and reading what is going on in the book has made me more courageous in bringing up subjects. Something that would sound so awkward to just confront Leslie about is so easy to do when we run across a delicate subject in a book. Now I feel comfortable stopping while we are reading a book together and saying, "Do you think we could talk about this?" or "Do you really know what that means?" I think it goes back to having the structured time of reading and talking within boundaries and yet being free to say, "Well, this is how I feel" or "This is what I would do." Hopefully because we have taken time now within the boundaries we set aside for reading, we can find it easier to come to one another during other times. It has opened a door no parent wants to close.

Communication Is a Two-Way Street

Geri says that book-sharing conversations have opened a new door to communication with her child. She was able to open that door not only because she used these conversations to communicate her opinions, reactions and beliefs to her child, but also because she learned how to practice active listening techniques. Using these techniques enabled her to draw out her child and tune into her child's feelings.

In order to understand our children, we have to try to understand how they feel. There are times when each of us hears only the content of our kid's conversation and thus we fail to tune into the feelings the child is trying to express. These feelings are often the main issue. Use reflective listening to bring that main issue of the feelings behind the message into the conversation. Relying on a simple strategy like rephrasing your child's statement can give both of you a chance to examine the feelings behind the words. Using this rephrasing technique will also reassure your child that you are actually understanding what he says. Consider this exchange:

Son: I hate Gary. He invited everybody to his party except me.

Father: Sounds like you really don't like Gary because he didn't ask you to his party.

Son: Well, no. I really like him because he was my best friend, and I wanted to go to his party.

Father: So your feelings are hurt and you are a little angry because you weren't invited to your friend's party?

At this point the conversation could go in many different directions, but the groundwork is laid for the father to understand some of the feelings his son is experiencing. By rephrasing his son's statements, the father invites the boy to elaborate on and talk more about his feelings. His father's active listening probably helped the son understand his own feelings better, too. A similar principle should prevail in book discussions: listen to your children and listen for their feelings as well as for the content of their statements. If your conversations are to be successful, each of you has to listen as much as he or she talks.

Most parents see talking to and with their children as a way of strengthening the parent/child bond and of encouraging their children's emotional, social, and intellectual growth. By helping our children learn to name and better understand the feelings that influence their behavior, we lead them toward self-awareness and maturity. By helping them learn to express their feelings and thoughts to others, we nurture their social skills. And by helping our children learn to articulate their ideas and opinions, we enable them to become more successful students and more independent, creative thinkers.

Every Parent Is a Model Parent

We communicate with and influence our children not only by what we say but also by what we do. In many respects our actions speak louder than our words. This is really not surprising since, from the very beginning of their lives, children imitate what they see and hear. They learn to speak by imitating the speech around them, and they learn how to interact with others by imitating their parents. As your child's earliest and most influential teacher, you are continually setting an example for her to follow.

The parent who admonishes his child by saying "Do as I say, not as I do" is underestimating the powerful influence of his actions on his child's behavior and development. For instance, by letting your child see you read books, magazines, and newspapers, you let her know that reading is an enjoyable and worthwhile activity. When she sees important adults like Mom and Dad reading for fun, your child is encouraged to think of books and reading in positive ways.

We also communicate messages about books and learning by the things we put in our homes. A home that contains a variety of books and magazines lets children know that reading is a regular way of communicating with other people and learning about the world. A home without books sends just the opposite message. You may feel that you can't afford to fill your home with books. But you don't need a large family income to provide your family with interesting reading materials. All you really need is a library card that will allow you and your children to borrow and bring home books from your local library.

As your child matures, book sharing can help you keep in touch with the person she is becoming. Sidenia Moses, a middle-school teacher who ran a family book-sharing program for her students and their parents, says that parents in her group especially appreciated this benefit of the program:

> At the end of one of our formal meetings, this father shared with the group that he felt this [family book sharing] had been the single most important way that he had gotten to know his

daughter. He felt that discussing these books with his daughter had helped him to understand and attend to his eleven-year-old daughter. He realized that she was growing up, and he was concerned about her different thoughts as she grows older. This father shared that he and his daughter have a good relationship, but he was "looking ahead." He wanted to make sure that his daughter didn't stop communicating with him.

Family book sharing can also provide you and your child with a way to look ahead and forestall breakdowns in your close relationship.

CHAPTER II

FINDING TIME— THE OLD BUGABOO

There wasn't enough quality time in our lives. This time that we spent together was the quality that we needed.

—A mother

Reading with your child does take time, but I always have time when it comes to my kids— especially if it can help my kids.

—Patricia Lovelace,
a reading teacher

The philosopher George Santayana once said, "A child educated only at school is an uneducated child." In the last few years, American educators have echoed that message again and again. These educators have been insisting that parents can make a difference in their children's academic success by becoming actively involved in their kids' school work and school activities. In addition to increasing children's success in the classroom, educators say that parent involvement has these further benefits:

- Communication between home and school, parent and teacher, improves.

- Parents discover they do have the skills to help their children learn.

- As school becomes a shared experience, parents become closer to their children.

Young children generally take cues from their parents. If we are interested and actively involved in school and school activities, then our children are more likely to follow our lead and take a greater interest in their own school work. In the area of reading, parents have an especially powerful influence over their children's academic interest and achievement. We can send our children positive messages about reading just by keeping reading materials at home and by letting our children see us reading books, magazines, newspapers, comic books— whatever kinds of texts we find useful and enjoyable.

We can also supplement the formal reading instruction our children get at school by making an effort to read with them at home. Jim Scott, a television reporter, has noticed that sharing books with his son has had the kinds of benefits educators predict parent involvement will and should have for children: "I have seen an improvement in grades and certainly an improvement in interest. It kind of sneaks up on you because you're reading and because you're enjoying it—suddenly you realize that you may be learning something as well." Most reading experts agree that parents can make a crucial difference in their children's educational progress (whether the child is five or fourteen) just by reading to and with them. Despite this fact, a recent government survey showed that only 35% of children aged 3-8 are read to regularly by their parents. Only one-third of American parents take time to read to and with their children!

By the time children reach the middle grades (ages 12-14) 90% of their parents have withdrawn from any conversation about school and books. That means that most parents do not talk with their children about one of the most important influences in those children's lives. During the critical transitional period from childhood to young adulthood—at a time when young people most emphatically need the reassurance and support of their parents and their community—a breakdown in family communication generally occurs. As a result, parents become less of an influence on their children's teenage development. Regular family book sharing can be a way to keep the channels of communication open during this time when peer-group values tend to carry more weight than the opinions of parents and teachers do. Fifth-grader Leslie Bradford points this out when she says,

> Before we started this, my mom and I kept away from each other a lot. If I had questions about something, I might ask my mom, but I would ask my friends, too. They would say something entirely different from what my mom said. This sometimes caused trouble for my mom and me. I feel more comfortable coming to my mom now. I might ask my friends about things, but my mom's opinion is important now.

Times Have Changed

The current cry for parental involvement comes along when most parents wish there were more than 24 hours in an average day. Hard economic realities and widespread acknowledgement that a woman doesn't need to be a full-time homemaker in order to be a good mother have caused changes in the structure of our families. In fact, the June and

Ward Cleaver model of the typical American family is no longer the norm. Today only 7% of American children live in a two-parent home that has only one wage earner. Now nearly three-quarters of women who have school-age children work outside their homes, and 25% of all children who are under the age of 18 live in single-parent households.

Between holding down a job, keeping a household together, and running the family "taxi" service, most parents find themselves wondering where to come up with a relaxed half hour to spend a little quiet and personal time with one of their children. If you are one of these parents, you know that becoming involved in your child's education by volunteering an occasional afternoon in his classroom or by devoting an evening to a PTA meeting would take some pretty fancy juggling on your part. But that's not the kind of parent involvement we're discussing in this book: we want you to carve a small bit of time out of your day and use that time to read and converse with your child.

Getting Started: Just Do It

Charlotte Smith, a mother who works as a financial manager, emphasizes how pressed for time most parents are when she says, "With both parents working outside the home and many times with single-parent families, you think you just can't take one more thing on." Charlotte goes on to say, "But family book sharing does not require a lot of extra time—you don't have to sit down and spend hours with this." Another mother who has been sharing and discussing books with her son for a year now says, "This program doesn't take much time for a working parent. This wasn't work. We just had a good time."

Everyone is busy, yet we always find time to do what we think is important. The first thing parents can do is just get started; just do it. Don't let yourself get distracted by an extensive analysis of whether you have time. Try book sharing with your child. You may find that it has an energy all its own. You won't have to engage in a detailed analysis of your schedule. It may take care of itself. Just begin.

Parents who make time to share and talk about books with their children discover that reading for pleasure with their kids is a way of strengthening family relationships and getting to know their children better. Kevin McKay, a pharmacist, says that what he found most beneficial about family book sharing was being able to tune into and appreciate his daughter Summer's feelings. He said the program really brought them close in that way. By now, you have all kinds of motivation to act. Why not ask your child to select a book he or she wants to read, and then you read it too? As the television commercial used to say: "Try it. You'll like it."

Set Aside Family Time

Every parent knows that family activities strengthen family bonds. What did your parents use to do to make you feel that you were an important part of the family? If you are like me, you treasure those memories that gave you a special sense of belonging. When you were a kid, what kinds of things did you and your mom or dad do together that influenced you? From my own childhood two types of family activities stand out in my memory—picnics and storytelling. Sunday was a family day for us. After church during the winter months, we often had a noon meal with relatives and then played games with cousins or aunts and uncles. During the summer months, we spent Sunday afternoons in the park eating picnic food and playing baseball or other active games.

Storytelling in our family began as an extension of homework. My mother would help us with our various homework activities by asking us questions, drilling us on math or spelling, or listening to us read. As a reward for getting our work done, she promised to read us a story while we had our bedtime cookies and milk. Yes, our bedtime routine really did include cookies and milk.

My father would arrive home from work at about the time story reading would occur (he worked in a grocery store and didn't get home until 8 p.m.). Instead of reading to us, he would tell us stories that came out of his youth in the mountains of Eastern Kentucky. Then he would say, "I'll tell you a story tonight, but you have to tell me one tomorrow." In that way he not only shared the fun of storytelling, he also got to hear about the events of our school days. We told him stories about the dramatic experiences we had at school and on our walks to and from the school building.

It is only natural for me to hope that my children will have fond memories of our family activities, but the significant point here is not the memories of specific stories or activities. It is the kind of time that we spent together. My mother and father set aside time to be with us children and to share their thoughts and feelings about childhood, about stories, and about life. In turn, we felt comfortable sharing our own joys and fears. Our success at school also was not unrelated. By helping us nightly with our homework, my mother showed us an image of the discipline required to succeed in school, and she showed us that working together made it all a lot easier.

Before you read on, reflect for a moment about the personal time you spend with your own children. How much quality time do you set aside for them? What kinds of things do you and your son or daughter talk about? Is this time spent with your child a regular activity both of you can look forward to and depend on?

Have a Daily Schedule

Maybe you feel the need to make special time for one of your children. One mother and father told us they got involved in family book sharing for the sake of their middle child. They felt he didn't get as much attention as his younger sister and older brother did, so they made book sharing a special activity just for him. Mr. and Ms. Buck found themselves in a similar situation. When their son entered college, Mr. Buck took on a second job in order to finance their son's education. Ms. Buck felt that she could support the family by letting their younger daughter, Julie, know that she was also an important member of the family by making time to read and talk about books with her. Ms. Buck and Julie used the evenings Mr. Buck worked at his moonlighting job as their book-sharing time. For her part, Julie says that she enjoys having scheduled quality time to spend with her mom:

> I like the time that my mom and I sit down together. I just know that from six o'clock to maybe seven o'clock Mom and I sit down and read together. I can still come home from school and play outside or do homework. We still watch *Jeopardy,* too! We can probably do this during the summer, too. Maybe when we go to the pool and they have swimming breaks, my mom and I can read during that time.

Younger readers will get the most benefit from book sharing when it is a regular daily activity. Older children may be able to adapt to a more flexible schedule. The important thing is to have a plan. As Geri Bradford, a working mother with an elementary-school-age and a middle-school-age daughter points out, "To make it work, you really need to say, 'Okay, this is when we are going to do this'....Setting aside a definite time to read and talk together is the best way."

Finding time for family book sharing means both you and your child must make room in your schedules to spend a half hour or so a day of relaxed personal time with one another. You may want to invite your child to take stock of his schedule with you. On the next page you will find a chart that can help the two of you figure out what time might be best for you to read and talk about books together. After you and your child have a clear picture of how much time the two of you spend on various activities, you will be able to see where the two of you can set aside thirty minutes for reading and talking. Remember that changing routines often takes time. Don't get discouraged if you miss reading sessions now and then. You may even want to begin by reading once or twice a week and then work up to reading more often.

Daily Activities

Parent

Time	Sun	Mon	Tue	Wed	Thur	Fri	Sat
Morning							
Afternoon							
Evening							

Daily Activities

Child

Time	Sun	Mon	Tue	Wed	Thur	Fri	Sat
Morning							
Afternoon							
Evening							

Carpe Diem: Seize the "Moment"

Here are some strategies you and your child can use to develop a plan for book sharing.

- *Decide what's important.* After both of you have written your usual activities into the schedule, take stock of how each of you spends your time. Talk about your activities in order of importance. The two of you may even want to prioritize these activities by making a list that goes from most to least important. Setting up such a list with your child could require some diplomatic negotiation on your part. Your child may insist that all her television programs, even the reruns, are important, but with some careful persuasion, she will probably be willing to compromise.

- *Be reasonable.* Don't expect your child to sacrifice activities that are really important to him. It might be better in the long run to suggest that he reduce the time spent on certain activities rather than eliminate them completely. And we can't expect our children to make all the sacrifices. Let your child know that you, too, are willing to give up or to rearrange some things that are important to you in order to develop a plan for family book sharing. Marge Simic made just such a trade-off in order to show her daughter, Whitney, how important it was that they make time to share books with one another. Marge's favorite time of the day is early morning when she enjoys a second cup of coffee and watches the *Today* show. When she and Whitney took a good look at their schedules and discovered that morning was the best time for them to read together, Marge got a chance to let her daughter know that she was willing to give up a favorite TV program in order to do family book sharing.

You may discover that television is your biggest stumbling block when you try to find time for book sharing. Ms. Marshall says that her son, Kentowan, often finds it difficult to turn off the TV when it is time for them to read together. She confesses that sometimes she is "just as bad:"

> Sometimes I have to be the one to turn off the TV. I can't expect Kentowan to do it if I am not willing to do it. We do a good job of taking care of our kids' wants and needs and we have to be just as good at giving them the important things that they may not think are important...yet! Reading is part of everything and even though Kentowan doesn't like to read, he will read with us because he knows that reading is important...we know that we need to make sure that our child develops the habit of reading.

- **_Use Television._** But we can't always say, "Turn off the television and pick up this book!" Television has its positive aspects. Watching and discussing quality TV programs as a family can be a way of working up to conversations about books. Watching historical miniseries, biographies, nature documentaries, and science programs with your children can open up interesting topics of conversation and can even promote reading. Watching a TV adaptation of a novel such as _Sarah Plain and Tall_ may interest children in reading the book or in reading similar books. If you have a VCR, you can make use of the connection between dramatized and written stories in a way that will interest the whole family. Even young children might be intrigued by the idea of watching a movie like *Hook,* and then reading J. M. Barrie's original *Peter Pan* to see how the movie compares with the book. And just think of the interesting conversations you could have over Peter Pan's refusal to grow up.

- ***Start with short periods of reading.*** If your child is just getting used to reading for pleasure, you will probably want to begin with short periods (ten to twenty minutes) of time and then lengthen your sessions as your child's interest grows. The fact that you and your child are spending relaxed time together may increase her interest in reading. Set goals for your reading. Decide how many pages or chapters you will read in a day, and then work toward reading together regularly at least three or four times a week.

- ***Make your book-sharing time enjoyable and relaxing.*** As you read the beginning of this chapter, you spent a few moments taking stock of the kinds of things you do when you spend quality time with your child. You might take advantage of this opportunity to consider what you want to get and what you want your child to get out of the time she spends with you. In the best of all possible worlds, what would you want this time to be like?

Whatever else you decide you want out of this time, you will surely want this to be a relaxed and enjoyable part of your day. Make it an activity that both of you can count on and look forward to. Bedtime may be the best time for you, if you start early enough so that neither of you is too tired to enjoy it. Barbara Putrich explains why she and her daughter, Gayle, decided bedtime is the best time for them to share books:

> Our son goes to bed about an hour before Gayle. It became a routine for us. Gayle would take her shower and come down to the kitchen afterwards. Gayle has some medical problems so she needs to eat something at night...we would sit down in the kitchen and read and talk about the book while she had her snack and a big glass of water. We made sure we had at least 30-40 minutes to do this. It got to be something that we really looked forward to at the end of a long day—like taking a sigh at the end of the day. The kitchen may not sound like a real comfortable environment to read in but it worked for us....It was a quiet time and we even turned the lights low in the kitchen to make it feel more relaxed. We were able to work around everyone's busy schedule because it was fun for us. There have been many nights down in the kitchen that we didn't want to quit.

- ***Read wherever and whenever works best for you.*** You may suggest that your child schedule a break in his homework time to read with you. You can use the break to read something together that you will both enjoy. Or, like Treasure Sickels, you may discover that scheduling time to read in the morning, before your children go off to school, will motivate them to get up and pull themselves together a little earlier. Treasure Sickels says that she was typically yelling things like "Tie your shoes!" "Don't forget your lunch!" or "What do you mean you can't find your book bag?" at her children as they scrambled out the door to meet the bus. But scheduling time to read together in the morning at the breakfast table has changed her family's hectic morning routine. Because Treasure's children enjoy their time reading with her, they get up earlier so that they won't miss the story. Mornings are now less stressful for Treasure and her family.

WE'RE READING! COME BACK IN 30 MINUTES!

- **Be supportive.** Once you have set up a routine, do what you can to protect it. Turn off the TV. Intercept phone calls, or even unplug the phone. Tell friends who knock at the door to come back later. You can run interference with friends and neighbors by posting a message on the door that says "We're reading. Please come back in thirty minutes." That should bring a smile to the faces of your own friends and a pop-eyed look of surprise to those of your kid's friends.

Creative Juggling

You may discover that your household schedule requires some creative juggling if you are going to fit in family book sharing. Since most parents spend a lot of time running the family "taxi" service, you can take advantage of this time by asking your son or daughter to read to you as you drive to basketball practice or to the dentist's office. Use the time you would ordinarily spend waiting for the doctor or the dentist as an opportunity to read or discuss books that you are sharing together.

Most of us feel torn between the responsibilities we have to our jobs and the desire we feel to spend quality time with our families. Obligations at work, or the daily household chores that must be attended to often eat into time that we would rather be spending with our children. Sometimes it's possible to solve this dilemma by doing two things at once. Karen Lykens, a middle-school teacher who also has a son and daughter of her own, told us a story about a mother who felt like she was caught in this kind of bind. Karen said that this mother felt so overwhelmed by her responsibilities that she would come straight home from work and then tackle the household chores. Now she comes home and spends a little time helping her son with his homework. Then he reads the book they are sharing to her while she does the dishes or folds the laundry. This mother says she and her son are beginning to talk more.

If your work schedule makes it hard for you to spend time with your children on a regular basis, consider Henry Marshall's solution. He works nights as a technician for a heating and cooling company and he managed to come up with a creative solution to this problem. Henry calls his son Kentowan each evening during his supper break, and they talk about the book they have chosen to read together. Their discussions about the books they are reading serve a two-fold purpose: they encourage Kentowan, who is a reluctant reader, to read for fun, and they give his father a way to stay in touch with his son's day-to-day thoughts and feelings. Mr. Marshall says,

> When we started reading *The Contender,* we would call each other and start talking about the book. Now that's what we talk about when we call every night. We are saying "The book's good, or what did you think about this part, or I liked this part, what did you think?" Because I work at night, we try to have a plan. That's the only way any kind of situation is going to be successful....Even though I am away when Kentowan and his mother read, we are still working on this together. We have this plan and

Creative Juggling

do this sequence of reading and calling at night. I find that this way of reading together brings us together on the weekends. During the week, we worry about the day-to-day stresses. Weekends are more relaxed and we can "air out" so to speak. Weekends are a good time for us to help him and get together with each other and catch up on the reading that was done that week.

Tomorrow Is Another Day

As you set up and try to follow a plan for family book sharing, you may find it necessary to take a break now and then. Don't feel like you have to abandon the program if you miss an occasional session. One mother, Barbara Putrich, expresses this idea when she says "Family book sharing is a little like dieting. If you miss, you can't beat yourself up. You just try again tomorrow."

Even though you may need to cut yourself some slack now and then, you and your child will benefit from being able to look forward to spending regular time together. As Jerry Nugent persuasively points out, making the time to do this may be difficult, but it's worth it. Jerry says,

> Here's how I look at it. I'm only going to have Nicholas until the summer after twelfth grade. After that time he will be off to school or wherever, and he is as good as gone from our home. Surely for this length of time I can give up something because after the summer of his twelfth grade, it's going to be all my time. Eighteen or nineteen years devoted to Nicholas isn't a lot of time out of my life, but it is a lot of valuable time in Nicholas' life.

Bridges to Cross

The following chart illustrates how you can turn statements that set up barriers between you and your child into bridges that invite your son or daughter to read with you.

Making Sure Reading Is a Pleasure at Home

NEGATIVE		POSITIVE
• "Turn the TV off and let's read."	VS.	"This book I picked up looks interesting. When your TV program is over, how about seeing if it's a book we might enjoy reading together?"
• "Your teacher said we need to read at home so your grades will improve. Sit down here and let's read."	VS.	"I'd like to do more reading for fun at home."
• "I'm going to unplug the TV, and everybody is going to read from now on during free time at home."	VS.	"I'd like to spend time together at home. Why don't we work out a schedule for TV watching and other activities? We can set aside time to read together. What would be some good times for you?"

Making Sure Reading Is a Pleasure at Home
(continued)

NEGATIVE		POSITIVE
• "You are going to have to give up your activities in order to get this reading done."	VS.	"We spend a lot of time in the car. Why don't we remember to bring along a book we both enjoy? You can do some reading while I drive. Others in the car might get interested, too."
• "Here is a book that your teacher said all kids like to read. You are going to read to me. Let's get started."	VS.	"Keep an eye out for books we might enjoy reading together. There seem to be a lot of interesting new books out. I'd really enjoy reading some of them with you."
• "We're only going to read books on these lists or books that your teacher recommends."	VS.	"Magazines and comic books might be fun to read for a change. We can read a variety of things . . . whatever seems interesting."

CHAPTER III

THE CHALLENGE OF MOTIVATING KIDS

> I didn't realize the enjoyment [my daughter] Julie and I had missed before this program. We laughed and cried at the books we read. We shared our thoughts and feelings on many "touchy issues."
>
> —*Cathy Buck*

The stories I have been telling you indicate that other parents and children have found family book sharing worthwhile. You may, by this point, have taken time to assess your schedule, and you may even have managed to make room for family book sharing in your daily routine. Now that you have laid all the groundwork, the big question is, "What can you do to help your child realize that sharing and discussing books with you is something he will enjoy?" That's the problem we will tackle in this chapter.

Look for a Model

We have already talked about how children tend to follow the examples set by their parents. But let me say again that the two most influential things you can do to persuade your child to read and talk about books with you are to let him see you reading, and to create a home environment rich

with interesting reading materials—even if you need to regularly borrow hefty stacks of books from the public library to
create this impression. There is reliable evidence that even in
the most depressed economic conditions, whether a child
becomes a reader depends to a large extent on his contact
with a role model in his family who is a reader. Such a role
model can be anyone (a mom, or dad, or grandma, or uncle)
who reads and talks about books with a kid. Did anyone in
your own family serve as a reading model for you when you
were a child? How did your family influence the way you feel
about books and reading? An adult who is an active reader
can give something very precious to the children who look up
to her—she can set an example that inspires them to get first-
hand experience of the rewards reading can give.

An active reader does more than read a lot of books
and magazines. An active reader shows her involvement with
a book by her comments and by her actions. If an idea
intrigues her, she asks other people to think through the issue
with her. If she reads something amusing, she laughs or shares
the joke with her family. An active reader does not simply
hide behind a book; she shows her family and friends that the
ideas she reads about stir her blood and help her connect
with other people.

These images of an active reader tell young people that
books and the ideas contained in them are worth paying
attention to. That's especially true if the active reader is a parent or some other grown-up who is especially important to
the child. But the child's model may also be someone outside
your family. Perhaps this person could be a model to both you
and your child. Your model may be a common acquaintance

or a television personality who discusses books and magazine articles and tells how they affect him.

You can build an atmosphere that makes books a natural part of your child's life. Think about the books and magazines that were in your home when you were a child. What message did your home environment send about the value and uses of reading? You can create an environment that sends positive messages about reading and books to your child by

- getting your child a library card as soon as she can scribble her "name" on a piece of paper and by making frequent visits to the library. Even a toddler will enjoy having a library card of her very own.

- encouraging family members to give your child books as holiday and birthday presents or to subscribe to age-appropriate magazines in your child's name. The children's librarian at your local library can give you information about which magazines your child will enjoy most.

- making a special place in your child's room for her to keep her own or borrowed books, comics, and magazines. You can build a sturdy bookshelf out of a couple of boards and a few bricks.

- regularly reading aloud to and with your child.

- talking with your child about books and the ideas they contain or suggest.

Bedtime Stories Aren't Just for Babies

Moms and dads often treasure memories of the quiet moments before bedtime that they spent reading picture

Bedtime Stories Aren't Just for Babies

books and fairy tales to their young children. My two youngest daughters wanted bedtime stories until they were ten and twelve years old. They often laugh at their memories of my falling asleep while reading to them. One time when they especially wanted me to finish the tale, they poured water on my head to wake me up. Our nighttime reading and storytelling time became such an important ritual for all of us that I sometimes recorded stories for my kids to listen to on those evenings when I could not be at home when bedtime rolled around.

By sharing picture books with their toddlers at bedtime, parents lay the groundwork for those children to become recreational readers when they grow older. Even toddlers can experience the excitement of identifying with characters who are having adventures they themselves would like to have; even young children enjoy the thrill of building their own fantasy or adventure in response to a story they have heard. We parents generally teach and show our children that reading is fun when they are babies.

When children grow older, we tend to think it is no longer necessary to read to (or with) them. Ro Pape, a teacher and the mother of an eighth grader who was a reluctant reader, found that reading aloud to her son was the only way she could get him interested in practicing his reading. Ro told us that her son Tony was more than a reluctant reader—she said he was downright resistant to anything having to do with books and reading. Ro kept waiting for her son to naturally develop into a good reader, but it just didn't happen. By the time Tony reached eighth grade, Ro decided she needed to do something; that's when she started doing family book sharing with her son.

Since Tony was not enthusiastic about the idea, beginning to share books with him took a little insistence on Ro's part: she had to persuade him to read aloud with her. But after Ro had read one book with her son, he was still not eager to continue. Then someone in their book-sharing group lent Ro and Tony a copy of *The Land I Lost.* Ro told us that everyone in her book club had been enjoying and passing around this book which was written by Huynh Quang Nhuong about his childhood in Viet Nam. Ro's decision to take her friends' recommendations and try this book with her son was the key that opened up Tony's interest in reading for pleasure. Whereas his mother had previously had to cajole him into listening to her read for a half hour each evening, when they read this book Tony didn't want their sessions to end. He would urge her to read another, and then yet another, section of the book. Because this experience really turned around her son's ideas about reading (he began then to read for pleasure on his own and his work at school also began to improve), Ro found herself wondering where we ever got the idea that we should stop reading to our kids once they start learning how to read on their own. As another mother, Geri Bradford, says, "Family book sharing is a real positive way of continuing to share books with your children as they grow older." Most parents discover that subtle nudges are enough to pique their children's interest in sharing books. Others, like Ro, find that both insistence and persistence are called for. Sometimes these measures are part of motivating kids.

Tickle the Imagination

Ro and Tony's experience points out how choosing the right book can really boost children's interest in family book sharing. Finding an idea or an image that tickles the imagination is often the spark that ignites our interest in reading a book. Generally, you and your child will want to choose books that reflect her experience and particular interests. For instance, if your daughter is trying to figure out what kinds of things girls can and cannot do, you might suggest reading a book like *There's a Girl in My Hammerlock.* In this story a young teenager named Maisie Potter decides she wants to be a cheerleader. But when Maisie doesn't make the squad, she patiently waits for the next season's sports to begin and tries out for wrestling. Even though she is the first and only girl ever to make the team, she surprises everyone with her skill and endurance. Such a book might stimulate some very interesting conversations between you and your child.

Younger children who have just gotten a new baby brother or sister might be interested in learning about where babies come from by reading a book like *Boys Are Boys and Girls Are Girls* with their parents. Likewise, children who are adjusting to a divorce might enjoy a picture book called *Charlie Anderson.* This picture book introduces us to two sisters who have two different homes—one with their mother and one with their father and step-mom. Little do they know that their cat, whom they call Charlie, also has another home where he is called Anderson. When the little girls (whose bed Charlie sleeps on at night) and the young couple (whose house he lounges in during the day) get together, the cat becomes Charlie Anderson.

Kids say they like reading books about other kids who are their own age. They like stories that speak to problems and feelings that they are experiencing. Ellen, the mother of a middle-school student, describes how she has used book sharing as a way of working out the inevitable problems that have arisen from her daughter's natural need to assert her independence:

> I see this stage now where she is more indepen-
> dent and growing away from us. There's times
> when she is more aloof, but it's funny. She still
> wants us to read with her. She and I read *When*
> *Parents Drive You Crazy.* I really enjoyed this.
> We talked about people's interactions and how
> we think.

Leslie, another middle-school student, says that as soon as she "started showing signs of puberty," her mother went to the library and got a couple of books on the subject for the two of them to share and discuss.

If your talking and reading sessions with your child are to be successful, the books you choose to share must be ones he will enjoy—ones that reflect his current interests or help him understand his recent experiences. When your child discovers that book sharing can be fun, he will be more motivated to take part in it. But until he makes this discovery—until he encounters a book that really catches his interest—you will probably have to encourage him with some firm and gentle persuasion. You can help your child link reading with pleasure by saying "Let's read a few pages and see if we enjoy this one." In the next chapter, we will talk in greater detail about how you can help your child select books that get him hooked on reading. But for now, take a moment to consider what kinds of ideas might tickle your child's imagination. Make a list of topics that deal with his favorite pastimes or that speak to his recent experiences. You may even want to check this list out with your child to see if you have put together an accurate assessment of his concerns and current passions.

Tickle the Imagination

Create Cliff-hangers

One surefire way to motivate your child to read with you is to exploit her natural curiosity. Think of the excitement you feel when you get so caught up in a story that you just can't bring yourself to put the book down until you find out how the plot works itself out? Even in conversation, we are always interested in knowing how a story ends or in knowing what so-and-so said or did next. Writers of fiction who know how to exploit our curiosity deliberately lead their readers to the edges of their chairs with anticipation. The daily "soaps" constantly remind us of this technique as they bounce from one mini-story to the next, always ending the scene in a way that leaves us wondering what will happen next: "Will so and so break up? Will they get married? Will he find her before she marries the wrong guy? Will she get revenge on the witch who has ruined her life?"

You can use this natural human curiosity to motivate your child to read with you by playing up—or maybe even creating—cliff-hangers in the stories you read together. This can be an especially effective strategy to use with reluctant readers. Linda Lee says she tried using the cliff-hanger technique with her daughter, Jennifer:

> It was hard for her to get excited about a book. Family book sharing helped me see how I could help her. Our reading usually starts out with me starting the book by reading the first couple of chapters. By the end of the year, we were reading parallel. I would read a chapter and tell her a little bit about it, and then this would encourage her to read further on her own. I'd encourage her by saying things like "Jennifer, wait till

you get to Chapter 30. You're not going to believe what happened." She'd say "Tell me what happened." Then I'd say "You've got to read it!" This kind of encouragement would get her going and keep her interested in what we were reading...The best thing about being involved in family book sharing is that she is finally reading by herself.

You can "create" cliff-hangers in the stories you read with your child by inviting him to predict the next event. What does he think will happen next, or how does he think his favorite character will solve a particularly thorny problem? Having ventured a guess, your child will probably want to read on to see if he is right. Make a game out of predicting events—this can be especially challenging if you and your child disagree about what a certain character is likely to do. By playing such a game, you are not only motivating your child to read, you are actually helping him improve his reading and thinking skills. Predicting events automatically shifts the reader into a higher gear and makes him think more critically.

Use Competition

Tapping into your child's competitive instinct is another natural motivator. Some kids love the challenge of a contest. Who can finish first? Who can figure out the answer first? Becky Jester, a fifth-grader, says that even though she and her mother start reading a book at the same time, she knows that she will finish before her mother does. Ms. Jester explains:

This is a situation where Becky comes to me and says "Have you done your reading?" or

"Aren't you finished with that yet?" She's always asking me "Where are you in the book? You'll love this next part!" She will come home from school and share something from a book that she is reading in class. Becky will say, "Oh Mom, you've got to read this! It's really good!" That's been fun to be included in excitement like this.

Change Places

You may find yourself surprised by the extent of your child's knowledge of a subject about which you know very little. Exploit your ignorance. It can give your child real motivation to share and talk with you. Books that deal with subjects your child is interested in, but about which you are fairly uneducated, can give the two of you a refreshing chance to switch places. Your child will probably appreciate the chance to be your teacher for a change, especially if you show genuine interest in and respect for his knowledge.

Remember the list of your child's interests and concerns that you made a little earlier in this chapter? Take a second look at the list to see if it contains any items you might be willing to let your child educate you about. For instance, Ms. Marshall says that her son Kentowan's interest in boxing—a sport she is relatively unacquainted with—gave them a chance to switch roles when they read and discussed a boxing novel called *The Contender.* Kentowan had the opportunity to explain the vocabulary of boxing to his mother while they were reading and talking about this book. Choosing books that allow your child to be the more knowledgeable partner in conversation with you is a great idea because it really can open new lines of communication. It shows that you do want to talk and learn. And it lets your child know that you are not using reading as a club to beat him into learning something. As one father noted, "sharing and exchanging information enlightens both of us."

Knowing that this is a time when you will give her your full attention and really listen to and talk with her can also motivate your child to make time to share books with you. As a wise man once said, "When we are listened to, it creates us—we bloom in the presence of those people who give us their attention." So much of our interaction with our children takes the form of our tossing out practical reminders, trying to plan schedules, or offering direct "requests", that most children will look forward to having a regular block of time they can use to discuss what they think and feel with us. Leslie, a fifth grader who shares books with her mom, says,

> I enjoy reading aloud with my mom now. When I don't understand parts of the book, she is right there to help me understand it better. She gives me lots of answers, she listens to my opinion, and I listen to her opinion. Sometimes we don't agree, but at least we hear both sides now.

Create Opportunities

If all else fails, you can always resort to bargaining. Alanagh Pimlot, a working mother who has three sons, has found that offering one of her sons the option to extend his reading time by reading in bed actually motivates him to read more. Alanagh explains:

> Last year he had to go to bed at 9:00. This year he is going to bed at 9:30. If he is reading in bed, he can stay up until 10:00. But he has to

be in bed by 9:30. But staying up to watch TV is not an option. Doing something else is not an option. He can stay up until 10:00 if he is reading in bed.

The following suggestions may help you create windows of opportunity for reading and sharing:

- ***Limit your child's TV time.*** The debate about whether TV inhibits children's intellectual and emotional development continues. One thing is certain, however: children who spend all or most of their free hours in front of the TV do not read much. You can help by limiting your child's TV time and by watching and discussing her favorite TV programs with her.

  A national commission suggests that 10 hours a week of TV viewing is a healthy average for most children. You can make the imposition of such a limit less difficult for your child by helping her decide which programs she really doesn't want to miss. You might even find it helpful to get out the *TV Guide* and make a list of the programs your child wants to see in a given week. Or you could keep a TV log on top of the set so that your child can record what programs she watches and keep track of how much time she spends sitting in front of the tube.

  Talking with children about the programs they watch is one way parents can counteract the famous "mind rotting" effect endless hours of passive TV viewing can have on kids. Discuss programs in terms of plot and character, much as you would discuss books with your child. If you apply the discussion strategies we will outline in Chapter VII to conversation about stories you and your child see dramatized on TV, you will probably discover that you really can use TV to create a window of opportunity for conversation and sharing.

Laura

8-93	1. Full House 6:00 – 6:30
9-8-93	2. Bullwinkels Moose-o-rama 6:30 – 7:00
9-10-93	3. Beetle Juice 8:00 – 8:30
9-10-93	4. Hey Dude 4:00 – 4:30
9-10-93	5. Saved by The Bell 4:30 – 5:00
9-10-93	6. What Would you Do 5:00 – 5:30
9-10-93	7. Wild And Crazy Kids 5:30 – 6:00
9-11-93	8 Baby I'm Yours By Shai 9:00 – 9:15
9-12-93	9. Nick News W/5 7:00 – 7:30
9-12-93	10. Martin 8:00 – 8:30
9-12-93	11. Living Singel 8:30 – 9:00
9-13-93	12 Wild and Crazy Kids 3:30 – 4:00
9-13-93	13. Hey Dude 4:00 – 4:30
9-13-93	14. Saved By The Bell 4:30 – 5:00
9-13-93	15 What Would You Do 5:00 – 5:30
9-13-93	16. Loony Toons 5:30 – 6:30
9-14-93	17 Hey Dudy 4:00 – 4:30
9-14-93	18 What Would You Do 5:00 – 5:30
9-14-93	19 Loony Toons 5:30 – 6:00
9-15-93	20.

Limit TV Time

- *Avoid reprimanding your child for watching TV.* Limit TV time and make fun books available for your children, but avoid playing reading off against TV. Criticizing your child for watching the tube instead of reading a book will make him feel that reading for fun is a duty, like eating his spinach and carrots.

- ***Reward your child's efforts with sincere praise.*** All children want to please their parents and nothing encourages them to try harder than receiving praise and acknowledgement for their efforts. When your child shares ideas and books with you, let her know how much you appreciate it.

Solve a Problem

As children grow up, they face many questions and decisions. Sometimes you know exactly what is bothering your child; sometimes you can only guess. In the pre-teen years, for example, almost everyone struggles with questions about sexuality and relationships.

Peer pressure often worries children because they want to be accepted by their age-mates. Or your child may be worried about specific problems concerned with school success or with growing up. Though your child may not start up a conversation with you about his problems, he may be willing to talk about similar problems and situations when they show up in a book.

The range of children's books available today covers almost every childhood question. During the '80s, Judy Blume was the most popular children's author on the shelf. Her books are about kid's problems: moving to a new school, being overweight, feeling like a nothing, exploring awakening sexuality. Many other authors also target kid's problems— divorcing parents, homelessness, drugs, alcohol—as part of their stories. These books are popular with young people because they reflect the fears and the problems in their own lives.

That is not to say that parents and children should only read and discuss "problem books." You should feel free to use the entire range of children's literature. The point here, however, is to remind you that your child may want to read stories that involve the hurts and fears that roll around in her own mind. Reading about a similar event in a book gives her and you a chance to talk about these important feelings without having to make an explicit association with her own doubts or problems.

As you read and talk together, you and your child will also trade jokes, stories about your interests, the future, the past, what events and characters strike your fancy, and so on. Your shared book will give you a point of departure. It will give you something outside yourselves to talk about.

Bridges to Cross

As my grandmother used to say, "You will catch more flies with honey than you will with vinegar." You may recognize some of your own statements and phrases in the negative scripts presented here. When you recognize your own words on the "vinegar" side of this section, spend a few moments thinking about how you can revise them into sweeter invitations.

Unintentional ridicule can quench a child's interest in reading. Inviting him to talk about books can be a way of drawing out a child who seems to do a lot of escapist reading.

- "What, got your nose in a book again?"   VS.   "What is it that you like about those science fiction stories?"

Asking questions that test your child will not be very effective in getting her to open up and share her real responses to a story. Try asking questions that invite her to draw some conclusions and make up her own mind about situations.

• "What gifts did Sarah bring with her when she travelled to the farm?"	VS.	"Why do you suppose Sarah brought gifts for the children?"

Nagging your child to share books with you will only make him feel like you have assigned him another chore. "I" statements like the one above will let your child know that you are really interested in reading and sharing with him. Your enthusiasm might turn out to be contagious.

• "Read! You know you need to. Your teacher said so!"	VS.	"You may not think this is a very exciting idea, but I want us to try it and see if we enjoy it."

Avoid trivializing your child's reading interests, even if they seem trivial to you. Expressing respect for her current consuming passion will do more to encourage your child's desire to read than buying her a whole shelf of *Harvard Classics* is likely to.

• "Good readers usually read more than comic strips and Nintendo magazines."	VS.	"I think you are getting to be quite an expert on Nintendo games. If you were going to write an article for one of those magazines, what would you write about?"

Statements that belittle a child's interests will let him know this book-sharing business is more for his parent than for him. Inviting him to share his knowledge of a sport or activity that intrigues him will have just the opposite effect.

• "You are interested in wrestling, but I don't know anything about it. Let's get a book I know something about."

VS.

"If we choose this book, I'm going to need help understanding some of the vocabulary and situations. Will you help me?"

CHAPTER IV

GUIDELINES FOR SELECTING BOOKS

I was very surprised that my mom would want to read books that I like to read. But I was even more surprised that she actually enjoyed them.

—*Gayle Putrich,*
a seventh grader

What Makes a Book Interesting?

Do you remember what your two or three most favorite books were when you were a child? Do you remember what attracted you to those books? The book that I remember most from my early childhood is *Peter Rabbit.* My mother read that book to me, probably before I could read print, and Peter's story became one that I read again and again after I had learned to read for myself. There was an impending danger in the story. As soon as Peter decided not to obey his mother's warning about going into Mr. McGregor's garden, I knew something terrible was going to happen to him. It was worth reading that story again and again to relive Peter's attempt to escape Mr. McGregor and to avoid ending up as rabbit stew. Then, when he did escape, I felt the warm relief and the comfort of the cup of tea his mother gave him as she put him to bed early.

Peter's disobedience, the suspense of the chase by Mr. McGregor, the punishment of catching a cold, and the reassurance of mother's cup of tea all made *Peter Rabbit* the perfect children's book for me. It provided an adventure and also fit my moral view—kids who disobeyed their parents would end up in the stew.

My choice of books, like my choice of friends, naturally changed across my growing years. My early friends were close neighbors, and my early books were those that were handy, especially the *Golden Books* because they were also inexpensive. As my desire for adventure moved closer to the real world, I read the *Hardy Boys* books, which I borrowed from the library and got as gifts. My search for adventure led me through several series of books about pioneer heroes, and that quest brought me to James Fenimore Cooper's classic tale, *The Last of the Mohicans.*

What Makes a Book Interesting?

In high school, my interests had shifted to realism, to using books to mirror my own search for an adult identity. The book I remember most from my teenage reading is *Studs Lonigan* by James Farrell. Studs was a teenager growing up in a tough, working class neighborhood in Chicago. His struggles for a place in the real world helped me see that I was normal, that looking beyond the limits of my working-class neighborhood was not crazy, that my sexual desires were not different from those of a lot of other teens, that my confusion over social justice issues was reflected in the outbursts of this fictional character, Studs Lonigan.

Match Your Interest

Throughout my elementary and secondary school years, my relatives gave me books as gifts, starting with the popular children's books of the day. As my own interests became clear, parents and relatives gave me books to match. And that's the first secret of book selection—find one that matches your interest.

Maybe you, too, had different favorites for different phases of your life because your needs and your reading tastes changed as you grew older. J. R. Kennett, a middle-schooler who takes pride in the fact that he now enjoys reading "big, 700-page novels," describes the changes in his reading tastes by saying, "I mostly like reading science fiction books. I've been into science fiction around three years. Before that I was into mysteries."

As you reminisce about the books you enjoyed as a child, think about what it would have been like for you to have discovered and read these books with one of your parents. Picture yourself sitting next to your mom or dad (or your grandmother or grandfather) and imagine the conversations that could have taken place about this book. What would you have said to that important adult about how the book riled up your emotions or described adventures you wanted to experience? How do you suppose those conversations would have changed your relationship with your mom or dad? How do you think that kind of sharing would have affected your attitude toward books and reading? You might want to keep those questions in mind as we think about ways of selecting books you and your child will enjoy.

As parents, most of us say that we want our children to "have it better than we did." When my parents (who married and started a family during the Great Depression) said this, they meant they wanted to give us material advantages they didn't have. We all want to give our children the best of everything, but sometimes we get so caught up in trying to pay for nice things that we forget that the most valuable gifts we as parents have to give our children cost us time and attention, not a lot of money.

By turning your child on to the pleasure of recreational reading and by actively sharing that pleasure with him, you will be giving him a gift that will accompany him for the rest of his life. You will also be forming a bond between you. But in order for your child to get these benefits, you need to find books that catch and sustain his interest. In this chapter, you will pick up strategies that will help you

- make reading fun for your child.
- help your child develop good book selection skills.
- teach your child how to use the recreational reading "acid test."

Make Reading Fun

The first rule of recreational reading is a simple one: reading for pleasure must be pleasurable. Family book sharing isn't going to be fun for your child (and it's going to be a constant struggle for you) if your child thinks the books you choose to read together are boring. Especially if she is a reluctant reader, your child may have some initial resistance to the idea of reading and sharing books with you, but that resistance generally evaporates once a child comes across a book or two that "hooks" her. At first your child may not realize that there are different kinds of reading. Julie Buck says that when her mother wanted to start reading books with her, she "thought it would be just like doing schoolwork." Julie's mother explains:

> Julie is seeing that these books can be interesting and that they tell a story that she can enjoy. You don't get this kind of excitement in a textbook, and kids need this nudge or opportunity to understand that there are different kinds of reading. I didn't expect miracles to happen by doing this program, but I think that it has opened a door to reading that has been closed for Julie.

Your child will probably be most interested in books that reflect his experience of himself or address his curiosity about the world in which he lives. In the final analysis, your child is the best judge of what he will find interesting. For that reason, you may want to encourage your son or daughter to choose the first couple of books you read together. While he will surely benefit from your guidance, he will probably be more enthusiastic about sharing books with you if he makes the first couple of important decisions about what books to read.

After you have shared two or three books of your child's choosing, you may want to work out a plan that allows each of you to have a turn at choosing the books you will read together. Jerry Nugent says he and his son Nicholas have worked out a strategy that allows them both to explore their reading interests:

> We've read some books that I had a hard time getting interested in, but because one of us was interested in it, both of us were. There was one book, *Anne of Green Gables,* that Nicholas enjoyed; personally it was a difficult book for me to get through...but we did it. We talked about that up front. Once we start a book, we are going to finish it. We do have different interests at times, but we were able to balance those differences. Nicholas would pick one book and when it was finished, it was my turn to pick the next book.

Guide without Dominating

You may have to work through your own attitudes about recreational reading in order to help (or even to allow) your child to choose reading material he will find really exciting. Maybe you believe that when you read, you should be doing so to improve your mind or elevate your soul. Maybe you feel that fiction books or books that don't qualify as serious literature are really a waste of time. To the contrary, many studies support the idea that recreational reading

- sharpens children's reading skills.
- advances their critical thinking abilities.
- expands their vocabularies.

- enhances their ability to communicate with others.
- and even improves their math skills.

Reading for fun can make your child a better student. And he doesn't have to read the classics in order to improve his mind. In fact, he will probably become a more motivated and skillful reader if you let him follow his own interests instead of imposing your ideas about what you think would be appropriate reading choices. Learn to discuss recreational reading the way you discuss sports, vacations, or any topic for which you have a mutual enthusiasm and about which both of you generally make statements, ask questions, and perhaps argue a bit.

Sue Miller, who teaches eighth grade and has started a family book-sharing club with her students and their parents, says she has noticed that it is often difficult for parents to let their children take the lead in selecting the books they will read together. Sue acknowledges how many of us tend to push our own ideas about what makes for worthwhile reading on our children:

> I'm watching parents pick out books and I'm hearing a lot of "Oh, this is a great classic. My child should be reading this." They are picking up books like *Johnny Tremain* because they [the parents] are interested in reading it. I'm having a hard time not saying, "You should be choosing for your child's interests." When we talk about choosing books, I stress that parents should be choosing high-interest, exciting books to get the child started. This is the only way these kids will enjoy this experience...I am very concerned that parents are telling their kids, "Here, this is the book we are going to

read." Parents need to understand that, in order to get this family reading going at home, the child should be choosing the books they read together...That might mean parents have to read something that isn't a classic or that they don't necessarily enjoy. But if it gets the child reading and interested in sharing, then it's the right book for this particular time.

Most parents who have done family book sharing with their kids say that they are not only reading more, but they are actually enjoying most of the books they and their children choose to read. You will, however, probably discover that you and your child have different reading interests and you will have to negotiate ways to balance her interests with your own. But your greatest satisfaction in family book sharing will probably come from spending time with and getting to know your child better, rather than from immersing yourself in books that fascinate you.

In the description of parents choosing books for their children I've just quoted, Sue Miller talks about how important it is for parents to let children choose the "right" book. You may be one of those parents who discovers that the right book for this particular time isn't a book at all. The right kind of reading for this particular moment may turn out to be

- a magazine about one of his special interests.
- a comic book series.
- the sports page of the local newspaper.
- an ongoing comic strip.
- any other kind of reading material that sparks your child's interest.

Guide without Dominating

Kids know what will get them interested in reading. J. R. Kinnett, a middle-school student whose mom and dad have managed to make reading books and talking about them a real family affair by getting their two younger kids involved as well, has some good advice for parents who want to share books with their children. J.R. says,

> You can't force anybody to read, and I just don't think it's right to force someone to read something they don't like. You'll never get them to like reading then! You've got to try to find out what they are interested in—sports, hobbies, TV programs, or whatever you can think of to find out what they like. Then you try to find a book to fit their interests. And having someone to do it with helps.

Inventory Interests

Taking an inventory of your son or daughter's current passions and then filling out a similar inventory of your own is one way you can guide without dominating when it comes time to choose reading material together.

Making a list of your likes and dislikes will also enable you and your child to set some limits about what each of you is and is not willing to read. One mother notes that she draws the line at sharing certain of her daughter's reading interests. This mother, Barbara Putrich, says that her daughter is into Stephen King, whom Barbara "absolutely refuses to read." Even though their age difference means that Barbara and her daughter have different reading interests, Barbara says she knows that her daughter has "gotten a real kick" out of the idea that they can still find some common ground on which to choose books that they will both enjoy reading together.

Taking Inventory

1. What do you like to do most?

   _____

2. What is your favorite thing to do with your family?

   _____

3. What are your favorite animals?

   _____

4. What things do you like to collect?

   _____

5. What are your currently favorite
   books? _____
   magazines? _____
   comic books? _____
   newspapers? _____
   comic strips? _____

6. What kinds of books do you like most?
   - ❑ fairy tales
   - ❑ adventure
   - ❑ jokes/riddles
   - ❑ poetry
   - ❑ how-to books
   - ❑ romances
   - ❑ picture books
   - ❑ science fiction
   - ❑ autobiography and biography
   - ❑ detective stories
   - ❑ sports novels
   - ❑ books about growing up

7. Who's your favorite character to read about?

   _____

8. What do you like about that character?

   _____

9. What TV shows or movies do you enjoy watching?

   _____

10. What are those shows about?

    _____

The Right Choice Makes All the Difference

If you enjoy reading and if you read a lot, you probably use some tried-and-true techniques to select books you are pretty sure you will like. But our children haven't yet developed reliable book selection skills. Because they may not be able to do a good job of predicting what books will meet their expectations and reflect their interests, they need lots of gentle guidance from interested adults. Such guidance is so important because children who are unable to find books that absorb them often quit reading.

Both parents and children need to agree that it is okay to quit a book that is not interesting. Everyone loves a good story, but if we don't think the story before us is a good one, or if we don't like the way the author is telling it, then we won't be motivated to read. When children are unable to select enjoyable books on their own and when they don't get the kind of guidance that will help them make good choices, those children are unlikely to develop into mature independent readers.

If They Don't Pass the Acid Test, "Ditch 'Em"

Jerry Nugent and his son Nicholas say they made an agreement to finish every book that they started, even if one of them found the book uninteresting. That plan works for them, but unless your child has already developed pretty reliable book-selection strategies, you may want take the "acid-test" approach to choosing the books you will read together. Leslie Bradford, a middle-school student who is also an avid reader describes how the acid test works:

The reading teacher said that if you read twenty pages of the book and you still do not enjoy the book, then that is not the right book for you. It may be the right book for somebody else, but maybe it's not right for you.

Becky Jester and her mother think that the acid-test approach is the best one:

Becky: Mom brought a book home one time that we really didn't like. It was called *The Bear's House.* I told Mom about Mrs. Bova's [Becky's teacher's] suggestion for books like this. She told us just to "ditch 'em."

Mrs. Jester: I like that philosophy. I think when I was growing up, we didn't have an opportunity to pick books that we wanted to read in class. Our classroom reading was required and we had to finish the book regardless of whether we liked it or not. I can appreciate Becky's choice to "ditch" it. It was a good book, but it would have been better for Sarah, my ten-year-old.

When you and your child choose a book, agree to give it the twenty-page test (You may need to lower the page number to five or ten or fifteen pages, depending on your child's reading level.) If the book doesn't pass the test, "ditch" it and choose another one. Trying to make your way through a boring book just for the sake of finishing what you've started can have an adverse effect on family book sharing, as Barbara and Gayle Putrich discovered:

Barbara (mother): The first couple of books we picked up to read were excellent—real page turners. That kind of a start helped us get family book sharing started at home. But then we picked up the book, *The Day No Pigs Would Die,* and that one did nothing for us. Gayle, who loves to read, even commented, "Do we have to read this tonight?" I kept saying, "Oh, come on. Maybe we just need to read a couple more pages to get into it." Finally, one night Gayle closed the book on me and she wouldn't read it anymore. I even admitted that it was awful. I handed it back to her to take back and pick something else.

Gayle (daughter): I hate to give up on a book, but I just couldn't get cranked up over this one—too much detail. It took them three pages to describe what a coffee mug looked like!

You can create your own personal list of award winners by keeping a list of the books that pass your acid test. Such a list will come in handy when you or your child want to recommend a "good read" to someone else. Reading over your list of personal award winners will give you and your child a real feeling of accomplishment once you're three or four books into family book sharing. Your son or daughter might even have a good time writing short reviews of the books on your list. Aside from its practical value for helping others make good book choices, such a list could turn out to be a valuable keepsake of your child's growing-up years.

Developmental Interests and Books

Characteristics   Interests   Skills

AGES 3-5

Characteristics	Interests	Skills
Accepts what is in books and on TV as real.	Enjoys magic and fantasy characters; likes using language and word play.	Reads pictures to help tell stories; easily memorizes rhymes and predictable phrases.

AGES 6-7

Characteristics	Interests	Skills
Beginning to sort out fantasy and reality.	Enjoys stories about people and situations that he/she can relate to.	Able to figure out the "code" so that print carries meaning; memorizes patterns and relies heavily on previous experience with a book.

AGES 8-9

Characteristics	Interests	Skills
Understands the difference between fantasy and reality.	Interested in facts and information about "real" people and events.	Knows how to read, but lacks the stamina needed for novels; needs the support of pictures, clearly printed text, and familiar vocabulary.

AGES 10-11

Characteristics	Interests	Skills
Understands "time" and incidents in terms of "then" and "now."	Enjoys learning about real people and events that took place "a long time ago."	Able to sequence events and mentally organize information so that it makes sense; able to project self into real time and places.

AGES 12-14

Characteristics	Interests	Skills
Relationships are important; developing principles by which to judge others.	Enjoys characters that share same problems, concerns, and feelings.	Able to "feel" and empathize with others who are "going through the same things." Reading takes on deeper meaning.

Noticing how your children's interests in print and books change as they mature and acquire skill in reading can enable you to observe milestones in your children's development as readers. Personal experience seems to play as strong a role as academic progress in the development of children's reading tastes.

In the early years (ages three to five), children love fantasy and fairy tales more than they enjoy reading about how soccer is played. At this age they enjoy using language and delight in chanting predictable phrases and rhymes such as "Run, run, as fast as you can. You can't catch me. I'm the Gingerbread Man."

No one ever gives up the pleasure of fantasy, but as six- and seven-year-olds begin to sort out the differences between fantasy and reality they more clearly understand the importance of their family and of significant people and events in their lives. Thus books about sleeping outside, pets, and friends are interesting to kids of this age, especially if the books are written so that kids can read them by themselves. With their entry into the world of eight-and nine-year-olds, your children will become increasingly interested in using books as a source of information about real people and events.

By the time children reach the age of ten or eleven, they have developed a better understanding of historical time and are able to project themselves into times and places they know were real. They enjoy learning about people who lived in other time periods and under social and governmental conditions different from their own. That's the reason that biographies and historical fiction are popular with these kids.

Some time between twelve and fourteen, most children tumble and scream their way into puberty. Hormones drive most of their interest in romance novels, of course, but their critical thinking skills also take a major leap forward and enable them to develop principles for judging people and situations. Kids of this age want to read novels about realistic problems common to their peers. Hence Judy Blume's books about feeling unattractive, not being accepted by peers, and similar preteen and teen problems are the rage of this age group.

As the vastness of the adult world begins to open up to children in the twelve to fourteen age group, these kids undergo a transition in their reading preferences. Beyond romance and pimples, they see a much more complex world and begin to wonder if they can survive in it. What if they had been with Anne Frank hiding from the Nazis? Would they be able to survive a plane crash and stay alive in the wilderness as the boy in the novel *Hatchet* does?

No clear-cut boundaries mark one stage of reading development from another. Your child may have quite different reading interests and abilities from the ones briefly sketched out here. These descriptions only give you some general ideas about where to start and what to expect when you and your child begin to share books. Start with his interest and then remind him that he has to give you equal time later to discuss one of yours. This will enable both of you to gain valuable information and to get a loving peek at the heart of the other person.

In the next two chapters you will find brief annotations of books that are often read and enjoyed by children in the age groups we have described.

CHAPTER V

BOOKS FOR AGES THREE TO NINE

Melinda (a mother): Remember when you were little and we used to go to the library and you would choose your own books?

Emily (a nine-year-old): Yeah, sure. I always had to have at least one Dr. Seuss and one Tomie de Paola.

Melinda: Since you couldn't read yet, how did you know which ones were by Tomie de Paola?

Emily: I looked at the pictures on the front.

You can help your child select books that are likely to have an immediate appeal for her by becoming more aware of the kinds of interests and preoccupations kids of your child's age typically have. Thus you will become more aware of the kinds of stories or characters with which your child is likely to identify.

The following descriptions and book lists will give you a good idea of how children's reading tastes typically develop as they grow older. Rather than reading each description, you will probably want to leaf ahead to the sections that apply to your child or children. We have provided ages that generally correspond to the developmental stages described here. But these age indexes are only guidelines. If a certain developmental characteristic seems to describe your son or daughter, but doesn't necessarily correspond to your child's age, you may want to look for the titles listed under that description at the library and suggest them to your child.

Children Ages Three to Five

Developmental Characteristics	Reading Interests	Books
rapid development of language; active, short attention span; understanding of time limited to "now" and "not yet."	enjoys chanting predictable phrases, retelling stories, and repeating rhymes; likes books that can be read in one sitting; enjoys being read to several times a day.	• Goodnight Moon • Peter Spier's Rain • The Very Hungry Caterpillar
curious about own world; learns through imaginative play; make-believe and magic seem very real	enjoys stories about everyday experiences; likes stories that provide comfort and reassurance; enjoys stories that involve imaginative play.	• A Baby Sister for Frances • Nice Little Girls • William's Doll • Harry the Dirty Dog • How I Was Born • What's Under My Bed? • When the New Baby Comes, I'm Moving Out • Corduroy • Where's Spot? • Brave Irene • The House on East 88th Street

Children Ages Three to Five (continued)

Developmental Characteristics	Reading Interests	Books
takes pride in own accomplishments; draws definite judgments about "good" and "bad."	enjoys stories with "small" characters who show initiative and bravery; likes happy endings; expects characters who behave badly to be punished.	• Katy and the Big Snow • The Complete Adventures of Peter Rabbit • Madeline • The Little Engine That Could

Children of this age are generally very active and have relatively limited attention spans; thus they prefer books that can be read in a single sitting. Books listed here for three- to five-year-olds are intended for adults to read aloud with young children. By reading to and with your child, you can actually advance his reading readiness. Research shows that children who have pleasurable reading-aloud experiences with their parents are generally more interested in learning to read. These children also tend to master reading skills more readily than do those kids who have not been read to on a regular basis.

Three- to five-year-olds enjoy participating in reading sessions by listening to the story being read and by answering simple questions that require them to find and point out objects in the pictures or to identify characters with whom they are familiar. Young children especially enjoy hearing their favorite stories read over and over. Your child's familiarity with a favorite story will give you the opportunity to ask simple questions she will delight in answering.

At this age, children begin to develop a sense of time, although their understanding of time is often as simple as "now" and "not yet." Books are a good way to advance young children's understanding of temporal terms like "before and after," "then and now." Books that reflect this stage of development include:

- *Goodnight Moon* by Margaret Wise Brown. This classic picture book portrays a little rabbit's evening ritual of bidding goodnight to each familiar thing in his moonlit room.

- *Peter Spier's Rain* by Peter Spier. This wordless book shows how a brother and sister enjoy a rainy day.

- *The Very Hungry Caterpillar* by Eric Carle. This simple but creative picture book teaches the days of the week, how to count to five, and how a caterpillar becomes a butterfly. Each brightly illustrated page has little round holes in it made by the hungry little caterpillar. As the number of holes grow, so does the caterpillar.

Because a preschooler or kindergartner still sees herself as the center of her own universe, she tends to like stories told from only one point of view. Such stories are easy for her to relate to and identify with. Books that reflect young children's egocentric interest, thinking and behavior include:

- *A Baby Sister for Frances* by Russell Hoban. Frances is an engaging badger who decides that Gloria, the new baby, is receiving entirely too much attention. Frances packs her knapsack, says goodbye to her parents, and runs away—to live under the dining room table! Frances continues to want to be the center of attention, even on Gloria's birthday.

- *Nice Little Girls* by Elizabeth Levy. Jackie has a problem with her new school: her teacher insists upon stereotyping classroom assignments as "boy" or "girl" jobs. Jackie's liberated views help the teacher and class to realize that tool boxes and train sets are for everyone.

- *William's Doll* by Charlotte Zolotow. William's father wants him to play with his basketball or trains. William wishes he had a doll to play with. His brother and friends call him "Sissy", but William's grandmother says something else. The message is one that all children and their parents should hear.

Although at this stage many children are beginning to express curiosity about how things work in the wider world, they are most interested in their immediate environments. They enjoy stories about everyday experiences, pets, playthings, and family members. They generally like to hear stories that provide comfort and reassurance. Stories that fit these requirements include:

- *Harry the Dirty Dog* by Gene Zion. This cute little dog named Harry does not like soap and water, but he loves adventure.

- *How I Was Born* by Marie Wabbes. The author has created for young readers the essential introduction to the facts of life and love. In this picture book, a young child recounts the events leading up to his birth— beginning with his parents' first meeting.

- *What's Under My Bed?* by James Stevenson. Two innocent but slightly worried grandchildren are reassured by their grandfather's imaginative tales about his childhood. These make their worries pale in comparison.

- *When the New Baby Comes, I'm Moving Out* by Martha Alexander. Jealousy surfaces for a little boy as he anticipates the arrival of a new baby in the house. He worries that all the attention will be diverted from him. His anger is soothed when his mother tells him about the special roles and privileges of big brothers.

Partly because they do much of their learning through creative play, three- to five-year-olds like stories that require them to use their imaginations. The make-believe world of talking animals or toys and of magical transformations seems very real to this age group. Stories that encourage children to rely on their creative imaginations include:

- *Corduroy* by Don Freeman. This story of a teddy bear's search through a department store for a friend ends when a little girl buys him with her piggy bank savings.

- *Where's Spot?* by Eric Hill. Spot's mother searches every corner of the house for her missing puppy. The reader joins in this search for the missing puppy by lifting page flaps to find an assortment of animals in hiding! This is an excellent book to introduce household names, animals, and the concept of "NO."

- *Brave Irene* by William Steig. Irene's mother is a dressmaker who must deliver the duchess's gown for the ball. Irene's mother falls ill, and Irene must deliver the gown. She carries the huge box through a winter storm to make the delivery.

Children Ages Three to Five

- *The House on East 88th Street* by Bernard Waber. This is the first in the series about Lyle the crocodile. A family discovers a crocodile in the bathtub of their new home. When the Primms overcome their fright, they see him as the most lovable and human of crocodiles.

Preschoolers and kindergartners are beginning to see connections between actions and consequences and thus to draw conclusions about what constitutes good and bad behavior. They expect that good behavior will be rewarded and bad behavior will be punished in the stories they hear. Children of this age are also grasping a further connection between actions and consequences when they take pride in their own accomplishments; thus, they enjoy stories that portray small characters like themselves taking initiative. Such stories include:

- *Katy and the Big Snow* by Virginia Lee Burton. This is a story about a brave, untiring tractor whose round-the-clock snowplowing saves the city of Geoppolis during a blizzard. Katy assists the local authorities in pursuing their duties during the snow storm.

- *The Complete Adventures of Peter Rabbit* by Beatrix Potter. Imaginative children can identify with Peter Rabbit and his naughty sense of adventure and then sigh in relief when Peter narrowly escapes the clutches of Mr. McGregor.

- *Madeline* by Ludwig Bemelmans. This story begins a series of books about a daring and irrepressible personality named Madeline and her eleven friends.

- *The Little Engine That Could* by Watty Piper. This is the story of the little engine that smiled despite the difficult task ahead and said, "I'm not very big but I'll do my best, and I think I can—I think I can—I think I can."

Children Ages Six to Seven

Developmental Characteristics	Reading Interests	Books
attention span is increasing; interested in learning to read and write; expresses a growing sense of independence.	prefers fairly short reading sessions; likes short stories or chapters that tell a complete incident; likes books with familiar or predictable stories; enjoys tales of responsibility and successful ventures.	• Frog and Toad Are Friends • Little Bear • The Courage of Sarah Noble • Frederick • James and the Giant Peach • Ramona the Pest • Brown Bear, Brown Bear, What Do You See? • Polar Bear, Polar Bear • Leo, the Late Bloomer • The Cake That Mack Ate • Ira Sleeps Over • Grandaddy's Place • Good Dog, Carl
strong sense of justice; able to apply rules of "right/wrong"; curious about gender differences and reproduction.	expects "bad" behavior to be punished and wants the "good guy" to be the hero; wants answers to questions about sex and relationships.	• Curious George • Flossie and the Fox • Julius, The Baby of the World • Before You Were Born • My Pully Is Born • Making Babies • How I Was Born

Children Ages Six to Seven (continued)

Developmental Characteristics	Reading Interests	Books
able to distinguish fantasy from reality; more curious about a wider range of things; developing empathy for others and a sense of humor.	enjoys fantasy and likes to use creative play to act out stories; interests expand beyond immediate sphere of home, school, and neighborhood; begins to identify with characters in books; enjoys jokes and riddles.	• Where the Wild Things Are • The Amazing Voyage of Jackie Grace • If I Ran the Zoo • The Baggie B. • The Velveteen Rabbit • A New Coat for Anna • A Chair for My Mother • The Relatives Came • Three Brave Women • Where the Sidewalk Ends • Alexander and the Terrible, Horrible, No Good, Very Bad Day • Amelia Bedelia • Wilfred Gordon McDonald Partridge

Because six- and seven-year-olds usually have longer attention spans than they did when they were toddlers and kindergartners, they are able to concentrate for longer periods without losing interest in a story. However, their attention span is still fairly limited and beginning readers may have trouble sitting still for even a twenty-minute reading period. For this reason, they tend to prefer fairly short stories. They may also enjoy short novels when the chapters are complete episodes. You may discover that scheduling two or three short reading periods during the day is a better strategy than demanding beginning readers' attention for one longer period of time and risking losing their interest. Some books which meet this need include:

- *Frog and Toad Are Friends* by Arnold Lobel. Five separate tales show how Frog and Toad learn about the give-and-take of friendship.

- *Little Bear* by Else Holmelund Minarik. This series of books uses elements of a child's everyday experience (getting dressed, celebrating birthdays, playing, and wishing for things he wants) to weave short stories about a child-bear and his family.

- *The Courage of Sarah Noble* by Alice Dalgliesh. This story, set in colonial times, introduces eight-year-old Sarah, who journeys many miles from home into the early American wilderness with her father. As Sarah sets out with her father, the last words she hears from her family are "Keep up your courage!" Sarah faces the dangers of the forest while her father builds their new cabin, and then she must stay behind in the Indian village while her father returns to the settlement for the rest of the family.

- *Frederick* by Leo Lionni. Frederick is a tiny gray field mouse. While his brothers and sisters gather food for the winter, Frederick gathers the colors and stories and dreams they will need to sustain their hearts and spirits through the dark, cold winter months.

- *James and the Giant Peach* by Roald Dahl. After his parents die (they are eaten by a wild rhinoceros who has escaped from the zoo), James sadly resigns himself to a life of misery with his two aunts. But one day he drops a bag of "magic" under his aunts' peach tree and then notices a giant peach beginning to grow there.

- *Ramona the Pest* by Beverly Cleary. When Ramona becomes worried that her pretty new teacher doesn't like her anymore, she almost becomes a kindergarten dropout.

As young children develop into beginning readers and strive to master new skills like reading and writing, they are trying to be successful at what they consider to be adult tasks. Thus they are usually very interested in gaining adult approval for their new accomplishments. While they do need frequent assurance that everyone progresses at his or her own rate, they also need lots of opportunities to show off their new literacy skills. Books with familiar stories or predictable phrases provide six- and seven-year-old readers with material they can settle into and get comfortable with. Here are a few sample titles:

- *Brown Bear, Brown Bear, What Do You See?* by Bill Martin. Young readers enjoy finding out what brown bear sees on each page. Bold illustrations accompany the rhyming text.
- *Polar Bear, Polar Bear* by Bill Martin. Martin's charming read-aloud book encourages young readers to predict what polar bear hears on each page.
- *Leo, the Late Bloomer* by Robert Kraus and Jose Aruego. Leo is a tiger whose father is worried that Leo hasn't learned to read and write and draw and do other things that young tigers Leo's age do. With his mother's support and reassurance, Leo learns to do all of these things and more.

Children Ages Six to Seven

- *The Cake That Mack Ate* by Rose Robart. Each page of this book presents a verse that builds on and rhymes with the one before it (like the song "The Farmer in the Dell"). The repetition of the earlier verses encourages young readers to read the familiar phrases in the story. As readers progress through the making of the cake for Mack, they will be surprised at the end of the story to find out who Mack is!

Going to school and learning to read and write contributes to primary-school-age children's growing sense of independence from mom and dad. They enjoy stories of responsibility and successful adventurous feats. They also enjoy expressing their new sense of independence by self-selecting books and activities. You might suggest the following books to reflect your beginning reader's new interest in independence:

- *Ira Sleeps Over* by Bernard Waber. This is a sensitive and funny story about a boy's overnight visit to a friend's house. The story focuses on Ira's personal struggle over whether he should bring along his teddy bear.

- *Grandaddy's Place* by Helen Griffith. A little girl from the city is frightened by the strangeness of her grandaddy's rural Georgia cabin. After a time, the grandaddy's charm and warmth open a new world for his granddaughter.

- *Good Dog Carl* by Alexandra Day. After Mother steps out to do some errands, Carl and Baby get themselves into all sorts of mischief. But Carl puts everything away in time for mother's return and thus earns the words of praise, "Good Dog, Carl." This wordless book invites children to tell the story the pictures portray.

While six- and seven-year-olds still enjoy fantasy, they are becoming more capable of distinguishing fantasy from reality. They are also learning to appreciate and experiment with the power of their own imaginations. Books that illustrate the power of imagination include:

- *Where the Wild Things Are* by Maurice Sendak. When he is sent to bed without his supper for behaving like a "wild thing," Max imagines a world of wild things in which he is king.

- *The Amazing Voyage of Jackie Grace* by Matt Faulkner. Jackie climbs into the bathtub, and his imagination carries him away. Jackie's bathtub becomes his sailing vessel where he confronts pirates and fierce storms at sea.

- *If I Ran the Zoo* by Dr. Seuss. Gerald McGrew makes up animals to live in his imaginary zoo. Everything from Gherkins and Seersuckers to Thwerlls and Chuggs can be found in Gerald's zoo.

- *The Maggie B.* by Irene Haas. Before going to bed, Margaret wishes on a star for her own little ship, then falls asleep. When she wakes up, she and her brother James are on board the Maggie B.

By the time kids get to be six or seven years old, they have begun to expand their sphere of interest and involvement. When they were very young children, their world revolved primarily around what happened at home and within their own families. And while they continue to need the support of close family relationships, kids at this stage of development tend to extend their interests out into their neighborhoods and school communities. They begin to develop a stronger capacity to empathize with and express caring and understanding for others. Thus these young readers often enjoy opportunities to respond to book-sharing questions that require them to empathize with the characters in a book. Questions like "What would you have done in so-and-so's place?" or "How do you think Rabbit felt about the boy?" give them these kinds of opportunities. Books that provide such opportunities include:

- *The Velveteen Rabbit* by Margery Williams. In this classic tale, a toy rabbit becomes real through the love of a little boy.

- *A New Coat for Anna* by Harriet Ziefert. In this poignant story of hope and revitalization set in post WW II Europe, little Anna and her mother must trade their possessions for materials to make the young girl a winter coat.

- *A Chair for My Mother* by Vera Williams. This is a moving story about a family's dream to save enough money to buy a beautiful easy chair after a fire destroys all of their furniture.

- *The Relatives Came* by Cynthia Rylant. A young boy tells this warm story about the time when a carload of his relatives came to visit from Virginia. Charmingly amusing illustrations show how much fun the visit was for everyone.

- *Three Brave Women* by C.L.G. Martin. While sitting on the front porch swing with Mama and Grammy, Caitlin screeches that she hates Billy Huxley because she thinks he will tell everyone she is afraid of spiders and that she wears underpants that have pictures of ducks on them. After Caitlin expresses her fears, she, Mama, and Grammy hatch a plot to put Billy Huxley in his place.

Along with their growing ability to empathize with others, primary-school-age children usually have a strong sense of justice, and they expect their understanding of what is just and right to be reflected in the stories they read. Six- and seven-year-olds' tendency to apply the rules of right and wrong regardless of circumstances leads them to demand that right behavior be rewarded and wrong behavior be sternly and quickly punished. Books that reflect these readers' ideas about right and wrong include:

- *Curious George* by H.A. Rey. George is a funny little monkey whose curiosity consistently gets the best of him. In every book of the *Curious George* series, this little monkey's curiosity gets him in trouble.
- *Flossie and the Fox* by Patricia C. McKissack. In this folktale a little girl outsmarts a sly fox by refusing to believe he is a fox.
- *Julius, The Baby of the World* by Kevin Henkes. Lilly thinks her new baby brother is disgusting. She cannot understand why her parents think he is the most beautiful baby in the world.

At about the age of six or seven, children usually begin to express new curiosity about gender differences and reproduction. Books that discuss these subjects in terms children understand can provide parents with a low-stress way of exploring these topics with their kids. Appropriate books include:

- *Before You Were Born* by Margaret Sheffield. This simple story helps very young children understand how a baby grows inside its mother in the months before it is born.

- *My Puppy Is Born* by Joanna Cole. Close-up photographs and forthright text show the birth and early development of a terrier's litter.

- *Making Babies* by Sara Stein. Designed specifically for parents to share with young children, this book deals head-on with questions that adults often find difficult to answer.

- *How I Was Born* by Marie Wabbes. This book speaks about conception with honesty and frankness.

Primary-school-age children seem to develop a keener sense of humor than they had as toddlers and kindergartners. They especially enjoy listening to and reading books with surprise endings, plays on words, and slapstick humor. See if your child finds the following books amusing:

- *Where the Sidewalk Ends* by Shel Silverstein. This popular collection of children's poetry looks at everyday life from a unique and wacky point of view.

- *Alexander and the Terrible, Horrible, No Good, Very Bad Day* by Judith Viorst. Alexander wakes up and finds bubble gum in his hair and from there his day only gets worse. This is an amusing account of a little boy's encounter with Murphy's law.

- *Amelia Bedelia* by Peggy Parish. Amelia Bedelia is a literally minded housekeeper who does exactly what she is told. See what she does when she is instructed to "dust the furniture" and "draw the drapes."

- *Wilfrid Gordon McDonald Partridge* by Mem Fox. Wilfrid lives next door to an old people's home. Many of the people who live there are his friends, but Wilfrid is special friends with Miss Nancy Alison Delacourt Cooper. One day, when Wilfrid overhears his parents saying that Miss Nancy has lost her memory, he decides that he must help Miss Nancy find her memory.

Children Ages Eight to Nine

Developmental Characteristics	Reading Interests	Books
wide reading interest and ability levels among individuals; increasing stamina for reading lengthier books; still enjoys read-aloud sessions.	enjoys uninterrupted time for reading; books provide pleasure and relaxation.	• Charlotte's Web • Sarah, Plain and Tall • The Littles • Homer Price • The Mouse and the Motorcycle • The New Kid on the Block • The Best Christmas Pageant Ever • Imogene's Antlers • Pecos Bill
peers are important; developing empathy for others begins to offer opinion and establish standards of right and wrong	enjoys books with characters (s)he can identify with; interested in exploring how "others" feel and react; interested in books that don't always have a happy ending.	• Danny the Champion of the World • The Indian in the Cupboard • A Taste of Blackberries • Ida Early Comes over the Mountain • A Dog Called Kitty • The Little House series
improved motor skills encourage interests in hobbies, crafts, sports, and games.	enjoys "how-to" books that provide practical information; likes to collect things; begins to look for books by one author or that are part of a series.	• The Encyclopedia Brown series • Matt Christopher's Sports series

As children mature and become more confident about their reading skills, their stamina for independent or silent reading increases. At this stage, some children may read with complete absorption, while others may still need lots of help recognizing words. Most eight- to nine-year-old readers are beginning to genuinely enjoy reading by themselves, but pleasurable reading aloud experiences with teachers and parents are still very important for them. Such experiences will go a long way toward encouraging these young readers to expand their reading interests and develop positive attitudes about reading. This is a prime time for parents to help their children discover that reading is an enjoyable activity. Age-appropriate books that generally hold emerging readers' attention both for silent reading and for read-aloud sessions with parents and teachers include:

- *Charlotte's Web* by E. B. White. As you read this well-loved story, you will meet Wilbur, the gentle pig, and the beautiful and intelligent spider who saves his life.

- *Sarah Plain and Tall* by Patricia MacLachlan. Anna and Caleb's father haven't sung since their mother died. When their father advertises for a wife, Sarah, who is plain and tall and who sings, comes into their lives and brings the ocean with her.

- *The Littles* by John Peterson. This is a series about "little people." The series centers on a colony of six-inch people who live inside the walls of the Bigg family's home.

- *Homer Price* by Robert McCloskey. This is a hilarious collection of stories about a small-town boy's neighborhood dilemmas.

As middle-elementary-school-age children become more interested in their neighborhood and school environments, the acceptance and opinions of their peers become more important to them. Children of this age seem especially interested in reading books that others their age have read and recommended. Sharing favorite books with their peers gives eight- and nine-year-olds the sense that reading is fun and has group approval. Books that reflect these readers' new interest in their peers include:

- *The Mouse and the Motorcycle* by Beverly Cleary. When Keith leaves his toy motorcycle behind while he goes on vacation with his family, the toy motorcycle becomes a real motorcycle for Ralph, the mouse.

Children Ages Eight to Nine

- *The New Kid on the Block* by Jack Prelutsky. This book filled with surprises, jokes, riddles, and giggles also contains over a hundred poems ranging from rhymed couplets to long narratives. The funny animal poems are surpassed only by the funny people poems.

- *The Best Christmas Pageant Ever* by Barbara Robinson. The worst-behaved family of kids in town comes to Sunday school and gets all the parts for the Christmas pageant.

- *Imogene's Antlers* by David Small. In this funny tale, Imogene wakes up one day to find she has grown antlers. After she tries all types of silly disguises, Imogene wakes up the next day to find her antlers have been replaced by a beautiful fan of peacock feathers.

- *Pecos Bill* by Ariane Dewey. As legend has it, Pecos Bill was a Texan who was raised by coyotes. When he grows up and meets a cowboy named Curly Joe, his legendary adventures begin.

We all like to read books about characters we can identify with—about characters whose personal qualities we would like to have or whose lives we would, in a sense, like to live. Eight- and nine-year-old readers are beginning to tap into this motivation for recreational reading. Being able to identify with characters in the stories they read can be a real motivational factor for these kids' interest in recreational reading. Their increasingly more developed capacity for empathy allows them to begin to put themselves in another's shoes and see the "other side" of situations and events. Providing kids in the middle-elementary grades with stories about characters with whom they can identify helps these children explore their feelings for others. As you read and discuss such stories with your child, ask questions that invite her to offer her opinion about differing points of view. These young readers' new interest in others may lead them to become curious about death. Readers of this age are becoming willing to accept some books that have less than happy endings. Books that reflect this stage of development include:

- *Danny the Champion of the World* by Roald Dahl. This is a story about an adventure a motherless boy and his father have together.

- *The Indian in the Cupboard* by Lynne Reid Banks. Omri's adventures begin when the plastic Indian he's been given for his birthday comes to life.

- *A Taste of Blackberries* by Doris B. Smith. When Jamie suddenly dies, his best friend must face the reality of death and cope with his great sense of loss.

- *Ida Early Comes over the Mountain* by Robert Burch. During the Depression, a clumsy young woman shows up to take over the houshold chores for Mr. Sutton and his four motherless children.

- *A Dog Called Kitty* by Bill Wallace. A young boy struggles to overcome his fear of dogs.

This is the age at which children typically develop interests in collecting, sports, and other hobbies. They like adventure and appreciate the continuity of reading several books by the same author—especially ones that extend a theme or a single story over several different books. You might suggest the following books to your young reader:

- The *Little House* series by Laura Ingalls Wilder. In this historical fiction series, the author describes the growing-up years of the Ingalls girls and the Wilder boys. Based on the author's own life, the books portray the hardships and difficulties of pioneer life in the 1870s and 1880s and describe the fun and excitement that was also a part of daily living in those days.

- The *Encyclopedia Brown* series by Donald Sobol. This popular mystery series gives the reader a chance to match wits with a clever boy. Mr. Brown, chief of police of Idaville, brings home all the cases his men cannot solve. At dinner he describes them to his son, Encyclopedia Brown, who usually solves them before it is time for dessert.

- *Sports* series by Matt Christopher. Matt Christopher's many sports stories include titles for young readers as well as for those in middle school. Sports fans will love Christopher's action-packed books (each covers a a different sport) about kids who must confront problems as they pursue the sport of their choice.

If you think your six-year-old will enjoy reading some of the books listed in sections describing books for older children, don't feel limited by the age breakdowns presented here. Likewise, if your nine-year-old enjoys reading picture books, don't discourage him. As long as the book provides reading enjoyment, it has accomplished the right purpose.

Chapter VI

BOOKS FOR AGES TEN TO FOURTEEN

I still like reading books about animals, and I also like the *Baby-Sitter Club* books, but I'm more willing to read other types of books now. I listen to the other kids talk about books they're reading. That helps me decide what I want to read next.

—*Julie Buck*

Remember those two or three books you mentally listed as your childhood favorites when you were reading the first few paragraphs of Chapter IV? Surely you liked those books so much because they portrayed characters or situations with which you could identify. Wendy Shlemeyer, a middle-school student, points out what an important element of book selection this actually is when she says,

My teacher recommends a lot of books to us. Many of the books she recommends are about kids who are having problems. If they are about problems that I'm not experiencing, they don't interest me. I don't want to read about kids going through divorce, or on drugs, or being sexually abused. These things don't relate to my life. I need titles that relate to some of the problems I am facing today.

The following book lists will help you and your child choose books that reflect her most current interests and relate to problems that are part of her present experience.

Children Ages Ten to Eleven

Developmental Characteristics	Reading Interests	Books
experiencing rapid physical growth; curious about all aspects of sex; trying to make sense of gender roles; forming ideas about their own and others' identities; increasingly concerned about "belonging" to a peer group.	enjoys books that provide information about gender roles; likes books that help her/him to understand personal problems.	• Are You There, God? It's Me, Margaret • A Solitary Blue • Park's Quest • The Giver • There's a Girl in My Hammerlock • Summer of My German Soldier • Roll of Thunder, Hear My Cry • Number the Stars • Homecoming • The Pinballs
challenges the authority of adults; critical of siblings and young children; seeks role models from TV, movies, sports figures, and books.	enjoys reading that provides insight into changing relationships; likes biographies of "real" people (s)he can identify with.	• Jacob Have I Loved • Dear Mr. Henshaw • Dicey's Song • The Great Gilly Hopkins

Children Ages Ten to Eleven (continued)

Developmental Characteristics	Reading Interests	Books
desires to test own skills and abilities; looks ahead to his/her independence; becoming more concerned with analyzing problems of the world; empathizes with victims of injustice and suffering.	enjoys mystery, science fiction, and fantasy novels; likes sad stories about death, illness, and other people's problems; enjoys survival stories about children "going it alone."	• Hatchet • Tuck Everlasting • Julie of the Wolves • From the Mixed-Up Files of Mrs. Basil E. Frankweiller • Across Five Aprils • My Brother Sam Is Dead • Lyddie • Shiloh • Stone Fox • The Land I Lost: Adventures of a Boy in Vietnam • The Westing Game • The Haunting • The Lion, The Witch, and the Wardrobe • Mrs. Frisby and the Rats of NIMH • The Haunting of Francis Rain • The Phantom Tollbooth

Selecting age-appropriate books for ten- and eleven-year-olds can go a long way toward helping them understand the rapid growth process many of them are currently experiencing. Although the rate of physical development varies widely at this age (girls are typically about two years ahead of boys), a rapid growth spurt usually precedes the beginning of puberty. Boys and girls continue to have somewhat different reading preferences, but kids of both genders typically become increasingly curious about all aspects of sex. At this stage when they are trying to make sense of gender roles, boys and girls are forming ideas about their own and each other's identities. Books that provide information about sex roles and invite discussion of gender stereotypes include:

- *Are You There, God? It's Me, Margaret* by Judy Blume. In this funny and always honest story, a twelve-year-old girl confronts the crises of adolescence.

- *A Solitary Blue* by Cynthia Voigt. A young boy thinks the blue heron is a good symbol for his life until he understands the importance of his father's love.

- *Park's Quest* by Katherine Paterson. Park has built an image of his father, who was killed in Vietnam. In learning the truth about his father, he learns much about himself.

- *The Giver* by Lynn Hall. A fifteen-year-old girl and her teacher are attracted to one another. Because of the teacher's honesty and concern, both grow in confidence and determination.

- *There's a Girl in My Hammerlock* by Jerry Spinelli. When Maisie Potter doesn't make the last cut in cheerleading try-outs, she waits for the next season's sports to begin and goes out for wrestling. Maisie becomes

the first (and only) female member of the team and surprises everyone with her skill and endurance.

- *Summer of My German Soldier* by Bette Greene. A
Jewish girl feels all alone in a small town during World
War II until she befriends a German prisoner of war.

Ten- and eleven-year-olds begin to place an increased
emphasis on the opinions and values of their peer group.
Thus, more than ever before, their book choices tend to be
influenced by the preferences of their peers. They say they
like books about "kids like us." Their concern about "being
in" and "being out" with their peer group can result in some
expressions of prejudice and in the deliberate exclusion of
others. Books can be used to point out the unique qualities of
different racial, ethnic, or social groups of people. Book-sharing conversations can also be a great place to clarify and discuss personal and family values. Books appropriate for this
aspect of these young readers' development include:

- *Roll of Thunder, Hear My Cry* by Mildred Taylor. This
is an unforgettable story about African American her-
itage and pride.

- *Number the Stars* by Lois Lowry. This story is set in
1943 in Denmark when the Jews are being "relocat-
ed." Annemarie must find the strength to go on a mis-
sion to save her best friend's life.

- *Homecoming* by Cynthia Voigt. A thirteen-year-old
travels many miles with her younger brothers and sister
searching for a home.

- *The Pinballs* by Betsy Byars. This book tells the story of
three children who have been placed in a foster home.

Any parent of a ten- and eleven-year-old typically begins to notice that his child's attitude toward parental authority and family relationships is beginning to change. Children of this age tend to become more critical of their parents and of their siblings. Book-sharing conversations can be a good way to keep the channels of communication open and to provide insight into changing family relationships. The following books (as well as others not listed here) can provide opportunities for both parents and children to "see the other side" of situations, events, and relationships:

- *Jacob Have I Loved* by Katherine Paterson. Louise, who envies her twin sister's talent and beauty, searches for her own identity.

- *Dear Mr. Henshaw* by Beverly Cleary. This diary of a young boy traces his personal growth from first to sixth grade. The diary tells the story of his parent's divorce, and how his relationships with them changed as a result of it. The boy also writes about how it feels to be the "new kid" in school. His diary also chronicles his changing relationship with an author to whom he writes over the years. Most importantly, the diary tells the story of the boy's changing relationship with himself.

- *Dicey's Song* by Cynthia Voigt. This is the sequel to the book *Homecoming*. In this novel, a thirteen-year-old girl takes charge of her younger siblings when her mother abandons them. The story portrays the children's life with their grandmother who lives on Maryland's Eastern Shore.

Children Ages Ten to Eleven

- *The Great Gilly Hopkins* by Katherine Paterson. Gilly is a swearing, self-sufficient girl who is in and out of foster homes. When she arrives at her next foster home, Gilly can't bear the huge and semi-literate Maime Trotter. However, life with Maime Trotter, from whom she learns to accept and give love for the first time, prepares Gilly for a reunion with her real family.

During this peak time for voluntary reading, ten- and eleven-year-olds especially enjoy stories about survival and "going it alone." As they look ahead to a time when they will be independent of their parents, they become increasingly interested in testing their own skills and abilities. Stories about children "going it alone" include:

- *Hatchet* by Gary Paulsen. A thirteen-year-old boy is the lone survivor of a plane crash in the Canadian wilderness.

- *Tuck Everlasting* by Natalie Babbitt. In this exciting adventure story, a young girl stumbles on the Tuck family's home in frontier country and learns their great secret.

- *Julie of the Wolves* by Jean Craighead George. With the help of a pack of Arctic wolves, Julie struggles to survive on the North Slope of Alaska.

- *From the Mixed-Up Files of Mrs. Basil E. Frankweiler* by Elaine L. Konigsburg. When Claudia talks her nine-year-old brother Jamie into running away with her, she chooses the Metropolitan Museum of Art in New York City as a refuge.

As kids in the later elementary grades try to figure out their own identities and gender roles, their search for values leads them to become more interested in the problems of the world. They typically have a highly developed sense of justice and concern for others. They also tend to like sad stories about death, illness, and other people's problems—stories that allow them to empathize with the victims of injustice and suffering. Book-sharing conversations which focus on the many aspects of right and wrong behavior are of special interest to them. Books that raise such issues include:

- *Across Five Aprils* by Irene Hunt. Jethro is too young to fight in the Civil War, but he watches his older brothers go off to join opposing armies. Jethro's family suffers as the neighbors seek vengeance.

- *My Brother Sam Is Dead* by James L. and Christopher Collier. A sixteen-year-old boy joins the Continental Army against his parents' wishes.

Children Ages Ten to Eleven

- *Lyddie* by Katherine Paterson. Lyddie and other factory girls must struggle against the unbearable working conditions in the Lowell, Massachusetts, mills of the 1840s.

- *Shiloh* by Phyllis Reynolds Naylor. Marty Preston befriends a stray beagle that belongs to a neighbor known for abusing his animals.

- *Stone Fox* by John Reynolds Gardiner. Willie enters his dog Searchlight in a dogsled race to help his sick grandfather pay off the back taxes on the farm.

- *The Land I Lost: Adventures of a Boy in Vietnam* by Quang Hhuong. This fictionalized memoir tells the story of the people, customs, and animals the author encountered during his boyhood in a small Vietnamese village.

Ten- and eleven-year-olds' emerging analytical and problem-solving skills lead them to tackle more complicated stories and to see book plots as puzzles their imaginations and analytical thinking skills can help them work out. They are also beginning to appreciate more subtlety in humor. Mystery, science fiction, and fantasy novels are often interesting to these kids. Books that reflect this stage of development include:

- *The Westing Game* by Ellen Raskin. In this wonderfully clever mystery only the reader has all of the clues.

- *The Haunting* by Margaret Mahy. Shy Barney Palmer is receiving unwanted messages from a ghostly relative, but he is afraid to tell anyone.

- *The Lion, the Witch, and the Wardrobe* by C. S. Lewis. Four children discover that a stuffy wardrobe closet leads to the magic kingdom of Narnia. This is the first of seven books called the *Narnia Chronicles.*

- *Mrs. Frisby and the Rats of NIMH* by Robert C. O'Brien. In this fantasy-science fiction tale, a group of rats become super-intelligent through a series of laboratory injections.

- *The Haunting of Francis Rain* by Margaret Buffie. Lizzie finds an old pair of glasses and is transferred back in time when she tries them on.

- *The Phantom Tollbooth* by Norton Juster. Milo embarks on an exciting adventure in a strange country of edible words and mysterious creatures as he visits the Kingdom of Wisdom.

Children Ages Twelve to Fourteen

Developmental Characteristics	Reading Interests	Books
developing a sense of identity is important; increased egocentrism leads to imagining self as center of others' attention and feeling that one's own problems are unique; intense interest in sexuality and the world of older teens.	enjoys stories of mythical adventures with heroic characters; identifies with characters who are intense or self-absorbed.	• Dinky Hocker Shoots Smack • One Fat Summer • The Cat Ate My Gymsuit • Motown and Didi: A Love Story • Stand and Deliver • The Goats
developing a capacity to reason and analyze situations and make value and ethical judgments.	enjoys books that reflect concerns about relationships with family and friends.	• Chernowitz! • Dead Birds Singing • Cracker Jackson • Izzy, Willy-Nilly
sensitive to feelings and relationships.	enjoys more complex stories and needs discussion/sharing time to negotiate meanings in stories that pose moral dilemmas.	• The Outsiders • I Am the Cheese • The Chocolate War

Developing a sense of personal identity is vitally important to middle-school-age kids. Books that help children "try on" different roles are of special interest to them as they make the arduous journey toward forming a sense of personal identity. They especially like stories based on the mythical journey or adventures of a heroic character. A new development of egocentrism typically leads kids at this stage to imagine themselves as the center of others' attention and to feel that their problems are unique. During the middle-school years, kids usually develop a new capacity for introspection; thus they tend to identify with characters who are intense or self-absorbed. Books that portray these kinds of characters include:

- *Dinky Hocker Shoots Smack* by M.E. Kerr. Tucker, the story's fifteen-year-old narrator, meets Dinky when he advertises for a home for his cat.

- *One Fat Summer* by Robert Lipsyte. This is a story about an overweight boy's quest for self-respect.

- *The Cat Ate My Gymsuit* by Paula Danzinger. A thirteen-year-old girl who is overweight and lonely joins a fight to help a teacher and finds friendship and a new sense of personal identity.

Especially at this stage, books can provide your child with insight into experiences about which she is curious but which she might not yet be mature enough to handle in reality. Middle-schoolers are increasingly interested in sexuality, in the world of older teens, and often in those experiences that adults forbid or disapprove of. Middle-school teacher Deborah Bova points out how adolescent literature can provide an education both for children and their parents in this regard:

> I try to make parents comfortable with some of these [somewhat shocking] books by explaining that it is probably better for their child to experience things in literature rather than in real life. If they are curious about gangs, drugs, rebellion, or sex, it's in adolescent literature and it's far better to have them read about it in a book than have their child go through a similar situation in real life. I don't [recommend] any books that I feel are damaging, but we don't read *The Bobbsey Twins* either.

Family book sharing can give you the chance to offer your middle-schooler the kind of parental guidance she'll need to balance the frank content of some adolescent literature with her own lack of experience in these matters. Books that reflect this stage of development include:

- *Motown and Didi: A Love Story* by Walter Dean Myers. Didi and Motown fall in love while trying to save Didi's brother from drug addiction.

- *Stand and Deliver* by Nicholas Edwards. A popular teacher inspires his apathetic, street-tough students to master college-level calculus and look to the future with hope and confidence.

- *The Goats* by Brock Cole. A boy and a girl are stripped of their clothes and left on an island in the night as a summer camp prank. Angry and humiliated, the two outcasts, or "goats," decide not to return to camp and instead begin an aimless journey.

Children Ages Twelve to Fourteen

As young teens and pre-teens mature and become more sensitive to complexity in human feelings and relationships, they seek richer and more complex stories. No longer seeing people and situations as either all good or all evil, they are able to apply ideas of relativity to questions about moral and ethical values. Discussions with parents can provide these young readers with necessary guidance as they try to understand stories that pose moral dilemmas and as they try to decide upon the values that they will choose to live by. Trudy Jester points this out when she says this about sharing these kinds of books with her daughter, Becky:

> I would probably have to agree with Becky that Izzy Willie Nilly was my favorite, too. I liked all the different lessons that it taught about prejudices and friends. In this story, the main character thought that her best friends would all remain her best friends after her accident. It was Rosamunde, the "plump and not-so-well-dressed girl," who became her real friend after the accident. When it came time to really be a friend, the others weren't there. There were lessons in this book about people and friends and real-life situations and circumstances that I liked—drinking and peer pressure, cliques, and all sorts of things Becky and her friends are faced with today.

Books that raise opportunities to discuss moral and ethical values include:

- *Chernowitz!* by Fran Arrick. Cherno tries to ignore the anti-Semitic remarks of the class bully. Action by his parents and the principal brings the prejudice into the open.

Children Ages Twelve to Fourteen

- *Dead Birds Singing* by Marc Talbert. Matt must deal with the death of his mother and sister who were killed by a drunk driver.

- *Cracker Jackson* by Betsy Byars. In this story, an eleven-year-old boy has nowhere to turn when his adult friend, Alma, gets caught up in a situation beyond her control.

- *Izzy, Willy-Nilly* by Cynthia Voigt. Tenth-grader-cheer-leader-nice-girl Izzy has been in a serious automobile accident, and her leg must be amputated. Izzy faces the loss of her leg and the challenge of learning to walk with a prosthesis, but her real challenge lies in dealing with her changed social status.

More than any other age group we have talked about so far, middle-schoolers like books that they can discuss with and pass along to their friends. Family book sharing can be one way for parents to bridge the widening gap between the middle-schooler's social and family lives. Middle-school-age kids say that they like books that reflect their concerns about their relationships with family and friends. Books that explore these issues include:

- *The Outsiders* by S. E. Hinton. This outstanding first novel about the tensions between two rival gangs in a city in Oklahoma is told from the point of view of Ponyboy, a young greaser.

- *I Am the Cheese* by Robert Cormier. Adam starts a bicycle trip to find his hospitalized father. Through the course of Adam's journey, the reader learns some secrets about Adam and his family.

- *The Chocolate War* by Robert Cormier. This story about a high-school student's psychological showdown with his classmates is continued in a sequel called *Beyond the Chocolate War.*

We hope the books listed here will provide you and your child with hours of enjoyable reading and many interesting ideas to talk about with one another.

Chapter VII

USING CONVERSATIONS TO SHARE BOOKS

We tried several different approaches to shared reading. We started out taking turns reading pages or chapters and then discussing them as we went along. By the end of the semester, my wife was doing most of the reading. It wasn't that my son couldn't read, but having her read to him was more relaxing. He didn't constantly look at the clock and watch the time. Once we found the right approach for us, all of us really enjoyed it.

—*Larry Cummins*

"I Hate to Read Alone"

You may be wondering why it's important for you to read to your child, especially once she has mastered enough basic reading skills to be able to read books on her own. The answer to that question is a simple one. Reading to your child (whether she is four or fourteen) is one more very important way for you to reassure, entertain, instruct, inspire, and just generally get closer to your kid. Darla Staley, a middle-school teacher who has started a family book-sharing club in her school, is aware of the important benefits reading to and with children can have. Darla awards those of her students who participate in the program with a poster that depicts Garfield, the cranky cartoon cat, saying, "I hate to read alone."

Kids' reactions to family book sharing point out the truth in Garfield's complaint. Julie Buck, a sixth grader says,

> I think another thing that made this fun was that I knew I didn't have to read all of the books by myself. My mom and I would take turns reading. Mom mostly read at the beginning of the books, but when they got interesting, it was easy for me to do some of the reading. Mom read until she got tired and then I would take over. We just shared chapters and didn't really worry about who was reading more. This really made it fun. *Sarah Bishop* was hard to get into, but reading it together helped me get to the good part.

Darla Staley also gives out a small reward to parents who participate in her school's book club. She gives them a bumper sticker that changes the usual question "Have you hugged your child today?" to "Have you read to your child today?"

Reading aloud to your child is one more way for you to give her your attention and express your love for her. It is also a way for you to strengthen your child's reading, writing, speaking, and listening skills. The influence pleasurable reading-aloud experiences usually have on children's listening skills is especially important. Because our ability to read and comprehend print grows out of our ability to listen and then process ideas and information, good listening skills serve as the foundation for good reading skills. Both skills are important ingredients in children's success at school. In fact, many educators feel that a large part of our children's current reading problems have their roots in a breakdown of listening skills. If you often feel that your child doesn't listen to you when you talk to her, you could find that regular and enjoyable book-sharing sessions will improve her ability and willingness to listen to you.

General Guidelines for Reading Aloud with Children of all Ages

- *Encourage your child to participate actively when you read aloud.* Reading aloud creates an atmosphere much like a conversation. If you watch good readers, you will notice that they often make eye contact with their listeners and often stop to ask questions like "What do you think about that?" or "What do you think will happen next?" Though the primary purpose of reading aloud is to communicate an interesting story, a comment or a question directed to young listeners establishes a give-and-take interaction.

- *Make it a family affair.* Even though your family may contain readers of several different ages and abilities, that doesn't mean that you can't enjoy sharing the same book. Bebe Kinnett explains how she and her sons and husband share a book:

  It's been a great family affair for us! Jim [husband] does most of the reading and the four of us sit around together and listen to the story. We've got two green rocking chairs that Jim and I sit in. J.R. is usually on the couch, and the two little brothers wrap up in a blanket on the floor. It feels like the old days around the radio or something. Then it got to the point where Neil [the five-year-old] would fall asleep every night while we were reading the book, so we started reading upstairs. We didn't have to carry Neil so far.

J.R., the Kinnetts' oldest son, elaborates on his mother's statements by saying,

I mean, when you think about the age difference in our family, there is almost ten years' difference between my little brother and me. So it's kind of like our interests range from *Little Red Riding Hood* to big 700-page novels. So I think that if we can do it, anybody can do it as a family.

Bebe says her husband got involved in family book sharing by default because she caught a cold and couldn't read to the boys for a few evenings. Since children typically spend the majority of their time with their mothers or with female teachers (90% of elementary school teachers are female) it's especially important that fathers take an active role in family book sharing. Fathers' participation counteracts the idea that books and reading are "just for girls."

- ***Don't let your sharing session become just another reading lesson.*** If you want your kids to talk to you, you have to adopt a conversational tone that shows you are sharing and not lecturing. Don't test your kids. Rather, make leading observations like "I wonder why this happened" or "Boy, that would scare me if I had been there!" or "If that had happened to us, how do you think we would have reacted?"

General Guidelines for Book-Sharing Conversations

The following tips can help you start book-sharing conversations with your kids and will also enable you to keep conversations rolling once they start.

- *Avoid dead-end questions.* If you want to start a conversation with your child, avoid questions that require a "yes" or "no" or a single right answer in response. Ask questions that begin with "how" or "why." Don't be afraid to ask your kid questions to which you don't know the answer. Your goal in these conversations is to share with, not to test, your child.

- *Repeat and extend your child's statements.* Often just repeating the last few words of your child's statement can serve as an invitation for her to explain or elaborate on what she has said. Or, you might pick up on some part of your child's conversation and extend it. If your child says something like *"Where the Wild Things Are* is my favorite book" you might say, "What happens in *The Wild Things* that makes it your favorite?" When you incorporate your child's own words into your reaction, you strengthen her confidence in her own verbal skills and you let her know that her opinions and ideas are valued.

- *Share your own thoughts and reactions to books.* Since our children usually take their first cues about how to behave from us, you can encourage your child to express his opinions about what you read together by voicing your own reactions. For example, if you and your child were discussing the novel *Hatchet* you might express a personal reaction by saying, "I wonder if I would have watched the controls and instruments well enough to crash-land that plane and survive."

- ***Define and reflect feelings.*** If your child is hesitant to articulate her reactions to books, you might help her define and talk about her feelings by making a guess about what is going on with her. For instance, if your child seems particularly upset by an event in a book, you might say something like "You look worried. Does this story remind you of your first day at school?" This soft approach is more likely to get a child to talk about her feelings than directly asking, "What's wrong?"

- ***Observe cues.*** Your child will probably give you hints that let you know when he is ready to end a conversation. When he starts staring into space or giving really silly responses, it's probably time to stop.

As you did with Chapters V and VI, you may want to read only those following sections that apply to your child's current stage of development. Each of the following sections

- describes how children at various stages of development typically understand and interact with books.

- offers suggestions about how you can get your child to take an active part in reading and discussing books with you.

- presents sample questions you can use to invite your child to talk about how characters and situations relate to her own feelings, thoughts, and experiences.

Reading and Sharing with Kids Ages Three to Five

Typical Reading Skills

Kids of this age usually realize that the story is revealed through the pictures on the book's pages. Because most three- to five-year-olds have not yet solved the print code, it's important to use picture books to start book conversations with these young readers.

Read-Aloud Strategies

Children of this age delight in being read to, but they also enjoy actively participating in reading and appreciate being able to tell a story in their own way. You can invite your child to take an active part in your reading time together by

- creating opportunities for your kid to correct an obvious mistake you have deliberately made. My three-year-old niece, Hannah, takes great pride and pleasure in correcting me when I make a "mistake" about a familiar character's name, or when I playfully change the story line of one of her favorite books.

- asking your child to retell a favorite and often-read story.

- inviting your kid to use information in the pictures to extend or make up parts of the story—to tell or read the story from looking at the pictures. It's not important whether her retelling or extension of the story is accurate or even plausible. Just listen; express joy; ask questions for clarification.

Reading and Sharing with Kids Ages Three to Five

Conversation Starters

Conversations with children of this age will probably be fairly short, so be prepared to ask your kid lots of questions she will enjoy answering. At this age, when children are still surprised and charmed by their own ability to communicate verbally, they enjoy answering simple questions like "What color is the hungry caterpillar?" or "If you were the caterpillar, what would you like to eat?"

Because preschoolers and kindergartners are developing an understanding of time, they like to talk about how they have changed as they've grown older. For instance, reading a book like *How I Was Born* might give you the opportunity to ask these kinds of questions: "What did you do when you were a little baby?" or "What things can you do now that you couldn't do when you were a baby?" Such questions are reassuring because they help children develop a sense of their own personal history and identity. These kinds of questions also help very young children more easily make the transition from being toddlers to being "kids."

You can encourage your child's creativity by asking him to answer questions that require him to use his imagination—questions that tap into his enthusiasm about the world of make-believe. For instance, if you were reading the book *Corduroy* in which a little boy's teddy bear comes to life, you might be intrigued by your child's answer to a question like "What would happen if your bear could talk? What do you think he would ask for?"

Children of this age also enjoy answering obvious questions about their immediate environments. They like to draw connections between characters in books and their own everyday experiences, family members, pets and toys. Because they are still enamored with their own ability to talk with others, they delight in asking and responding to questions to which everyone seems to know the answers. Questions like "Frances the Badger has a new baby sister. Do you know anyone who has a baby sister?" are a good way to invite young children to talk to you about themselves and about how they see the world around them.

Because preschoolers and kindergartners are beginning to see connections between actions and consequences, story-sharing questions that point out this kind of connection will be of special interest to them. Questions like "What did Peter Rabbit do to get himself in so much trouble?" or "How did the Little Engine get up the hill?" point out such connections.

Reading and Sharing with Kids Ages Six to Seven

Typical Reading Skills

Kids of this age usually know the alphabet and are often able to sound out new words. Six- and seven-year-old readers often use pictures as clues to help them make guesses about unfamiliar words. Children of this age love reading the same book over and over because frequent repetition allows them to memorize the story so that they can "read" it back to you. Developing this kind of familiarity with favorite stories will enable your young reader to gain skill and confidence through repeated practice and success.

Read-Aloud Strategies

Reading aloud to six- and seven-year-olds can go a long way toward nurturing their blossoming interest in books and reading. Children of this age justly take real satisfaction in their newly acquired reading and writing skills. So, they will probably be excited by the prospect of reading to you, even though they may be interested in doing so only for short periods of time. Try the following reading strategies with your young reader:

- Make a game of reading by asking your child to predict events in a story by looking at the pictures of a new book before you read it together. Listen to your child tell you what she thinks is going to happen in the story just from looking at the pictures. After you have read the story, the two of you can then talk about how it did or didn't meet your child's expectations.

- Encourage your child to participate in your reading sessions by pausing at points where you think she will be able to fill in or finish sentences. This is especially enjoyable with books like Dr. Seuss stories that have rhyming text or with books that have predictable phrases like the ones in *The Cake That Mack Ate.*

- If your child decides that she wants to read to you (and your book sharing probably will be more successful if you let her decide when she wants to do so) make sure you don't allow your sharing session to turn into a reading lesson. You can always help your child with her reading skills when it's time for homework. Make an effort to let her know that this is relaxed time you and she will spend just reading and talking together. If your child stumbles over a word or phrase as she reads to you, you will, of course, want to help her. Here's a good rule of thumb: silently count to five before you supply the troublesome word or phrase that has stumped your child. Correct your child's mistakes only if they significantly alter the meaning of the story.

Conversation Starters

People who are avid readers say that books are important to them partly because situations and characters in books help them reflect on or better understand their own lives and experiences. Conversation-starting questions that invite children to relate or compare their own experience or feelings to those of the characters in the books they read are appropriate for children of all ages. For instance, say you and your child are reading *Ramona the Pest;* asking a question like "Have you ever felt like Ramona?" or "Have you ever worried that someone would stop liking you?" will encourage her to make these kinds of connections.

Because beginning readers are widening the scope of their immediate environments to include the larger world of school and their neighborhoods, they like talking about their new independence. Reading books like *Ira Sleeps Over* or *Grandaddy's Place* might give you an opportunity to talk with your child about those situations in which his new independence becomes a source of anxiety, rather than of satisfaction. You can ask questions like the following ones:

- "When you are afraid, like Ira was in the book, what makes you feel better?"

- "Ira was able to talk about how scared he was to leave his blanket behind. Do you remember a time when you were scared, and talked to someone about it? What happened?"

- "Do you think so-and-so ever gets afraid? What do you think might scare him?"

- "What things do you get scared by?"

Part of your role in book-sharing conversations is to ask questions that will get your child to talk with you about herself. But once your conversations get started, your child will probably turn the tables and ask you questions of her own. When this happens, be prepared to answer in a way that encourages further openness so that she will feel free to ask more questions. Depending on the nature of the question your child has asked, this can require some fast thinking on your part. For instance, if your conversation about Ira and his problems with sleeping over at his friend's house should lead your child to ask you what you are afraid of, you will want to respond in a way that neither shuts down the conversation nor confuses or threatens your child. Putting yourself in your child's place by saying "Well, when I was your age, I was afraid of..." is a good way to answer questions like this. Such a strategy allows you to share your experiences without imposing adult concerns and anxieties on your child.

Asking questions that invite beginning readers to empathize with or put themselves in the place of characters in books encourages these kids to further develop and express concern for others. Questions like "How do you think the mother felt when her children gave her the beautiful new chair they had saved their money to buy?" offers kids opportunities to try to see things from another person's point of view.

Because primary-school-age children expect their own sense of justice to be reflected in the stories they read, they will probably be intrigued by questions that require them to think about good/bad behavior and its consequences. Asking questions like "How did Curious George get in trouble?" or making statements like "Curious George has a lesson to learn. He made a mistake, but his owner always loves him, just like I still love you when you do something wrong" or asking "What do you think would happen to you if you did what George did?" is a way of inviting children to formulate judgments and express their opinions about what they read.

Since children of this age generally take pride in their ability to separate fantasy from reality, asking questions like "Do you think this could really happen?" or inviting your child to rewrite the ending of a story by relying on his imagination is a fun way to begin a conversation. You can even introduce the idea of writing an alternate ending for a story you've read together by teasing your child with a "what-if" statement: "What if so-and-so happened? What do you think would happen then?"

Reading and Sharing with Kids Ages Eight to Nine

Typical Reading Skills

Young readers of this age are fully aware of the important connection between written print and the spoken word. That is to say, eight- and nine-year-olds usually know that each word they see printed on the page is a representation of a single spoken word. They can use clues they see in the illustrations and the sounds of initial consonants to decode unfamiliar words, but they are definitely reading the words rather than the pictures. They know that reading a book is a good way to get useful information.

Reading Strategies

When children begin to think of themselves as real readers, they are eager to show off their new skills and thus usually pester everyone within hearing distance to listen to them read. Ironically, at this stage most parents stop reading to or with their children. Just when their children have developed a new and vital relationship with books and are more enthusiastic than ever about reading, most parents opt out of the picture. At this crucial point you can do a lot to instill a love of books in your young reader. Ellen, a mother who has been sharing books with her daughters for some time now, explains:

> When I was a child, my parents never read to us except our Sunday School readings. That was it. But when I was at school, I developed a love for reading when I was in third grade. I had a teacher who read to us every day after lunch. She started reading the *Little House* books by Laura Ingalls Wilder. I loved those books so

much. And I think that's what got me started reading. I wanted to pass that love on to my kids so I read to them.

Try the following book-sharing approaches with kids ages eight and nine:

- Just because your child can now read independently doesn't mean you should give up the pleasure of reading aloud to her. Continue to read to your child and invite her to take over and read to you whenever she wants to.

- Offer invitations that are not open-ended, such as "Would you like to read the next paragraph?" or "Do you want to read a page and then I'll read a page?" But don't insist that your child read to you. If she doesn't want to read aloud, be prepared to do all the reading yourself.

- Invite your child to be an active listener by stopping frequently to ask him questions or to invite him to comment on something that has happened in the story. When your child reads to you, participate by interrupting to reflect on something he's just read or to ask a question about the way the story is unfolding.

- Don't play reading teacher. Just be a companion with whom your child can share and enjoy books. If your child stumbles over a word or phrase as she reads to you, help her. Here's a good rule of thumb: silently count to five before you supply the troublesome word or phrase that has stumped your child. Correct her mistakes only if they drastically alter the meaning of the story. Make an effort to let your child know that this is relaxed time that you can spend simply reading and talking together about stories.

Conversation Starters

Tap into your child's blossoming interest in what her peers think of her by asking questions that require her to consider different (and differing) points of view. For example, if you were reading E. B. White's children's classic, *Charlotte's Web,* you might ask, "What do you suppose the goose (or the sheep, or the rat) thought about Wilbur the pig? Whose opinion do you agree with?"

Even though children of this age are usually beginning to develop a new interest in peer acceptance, your child still needs repeated reassurance that everyone is different and that each individual develops at his or her own rate. You can nurture your child's sense of individuality by asking questions which point out the differences and similarities of characters in the books you read together. For instance, you might ask the following kinds of questions about *Charlotte's Web:*

- "How do you think Wilbur the pig's personality is different from Charlotte the spider's?" "How do they do things differently?"
- "If they are so different, how come they are friends and are able to take care of each other?"
- "Who takes care of you?"
- "Whom do you take care of?"
- "How do you think you are different from or similar to so-and-so?"

Asking questions that require your child to empathize with a character in a book can be a way of getting him to talk about and better understand his own feelings. For instance, in the book *A Taste of Blackberries,* Jamie's best friend gets stung by a bee when he and Jamie are playing together, and then the friend dies. In addition to feeling grief about his friend's death, Jamie is overcome by guilt because he laughed when his friend knocked down the bee hive and then got chased by the bees. Asking your child to put herself in Jamie's situation and talk about how she would feel if her best friend got hurt or got in serious trouble is one way of encouraging your child to define her own feelings and to talk about those feelings she has for other people.

Eight- and nine-year-olds often get interested in reading several books by the same author. This gives them the pleasant opportunity to become experts on a particular writer. Sharing books in a series with your young reader can open up interesting possibilities for book-sharing conversations. Conversations about "series" books are an especially good way to explore eight- and nine-year-old's increasingly more sophisticated understanding of how the past compares with the present. Questions like "Do you remember when such-and-such happened to Laura in the first *Little House* book we read? What do you think she would do if that happened to her now?" rely on the sense of continuity this kind of reading provides.

You can even extend questions of this kind into invitations for your child to tell you his version of stories from the past. Play the "remember when" game and ask your son or daughter to give you his version of an experience you both shared. You may be surprised to learn that he remembers it quite differently than you do. Having stories to tell about ourselves and getting a clear view of our own personal history is one way of saying "This is who I am and here's how I got to be this person."

Conversation Starters for Children Eight to Nine

Reading and Sharing with Kids Ages Ten to Eleven

Typical Reading Skills

Children in the ten-to-eleven age group usually can read independently, even though they may lack stamina for sustained reading. Young readers of this age begin to look to books for information about and insight into their own problems.

Reading Strategies

Because developing readers generally have confidence in their reading skills, striking a balance between shared and independent reading is a good idea with children at this stage. Try the following approaches with your child:

- Even those kids who are teetering on the verge of adolescence still love being read to. If you stopped reading to your child several years ago but now you want to share books with him, you may discover that he has some resistance to the idea. Be persistent: read high interest material to him or with him and do so regularly and for short periods of time. His enjoyment of a good story will eventually win out over his feeling that being read to is "just for babies."

- You can alternate roles as reader and listener by deciding to trade off reading chapters of the book aloud to one another. When you are the listener, make it a habit to interrupt occasionally to ask questions or to comment on how the story is developing. When your child is the listener, encourage her to participate in the reading by interrupting whenever she wants to offer her own comments and questions. Keep your reading sessions relaxed and avoid slipping into the role of reading teacher. Your reading will be more enjoyable and your conversations will be more meaningful if you share instead of teach.

- More advanced and confident readers will certainly be able to read chapters or sections of the book independently. If you decide that each of you will read the book on his own, you may want to make a habit of marking your favorite passages (small Post-It Notes™ work well for this) and then reading them aloud to one another when you come together for your book-sharing conversations.

- At this age, when kids are trying to make sense of gender roles, it's especially important that book sharing is a family affair. Fathers should make an extra effort to read with children. Because the vast majority of elementary school teachers are women, boys often associate reading with women and school work.

Conversation Starters

Most ten- and eleven-year-olds develop their own opinions—ones which may or may not reflect the convictions of their parents. It's important that you respect and avoid censoring the views your child expresses in book-sharing conversations. Simply expressing your own opinions is one way of doing this. You can agree to disagree by making statements like, "I understand and respect your opinion, but I believe..." If your book-sharing conversations are to be meaningful for both of you, you will need to allow your child to express views that contradict your own. Unfortunately, disagreeing with Mom or Dad is usually one of the ways kids of this age assert their independence and individuality. Recognize those disagreements as part of growing up, not as a personal attack that you will have to squelch.

Books that portray young characters who must interpret and unravel moral dilemmas can give you and your child opportunities to discuss important values. For instance, if you and your child are reading *Shiloh,* the story about a boy named Marty who takes in (and in effect steals) a beagle that belongs to his neighbor, you might ask your son or daughter to work out the problem of whether the fact that the neighbor was known for abusing his dogs justifies Marty's dishonesty. Asking your child to consider alternate courses of action is one way to drive home the point that there is usually more than one way to solve a problem. Asking questions like "What do you think would have happened if Marty had reported the man to the people at the Humane Society?" is a way of emphasizing the fact that all actions have consequences and that those consequences can often be predicted and considered before we take action. Book-sharing conversations that focus on the many aspects of right and wrong are a way for you to encourage your child to take further responsibility for his own behavior.

During this period when kids are figuring out for themselves what it means to be male or female, discussing gender-roles and stereotypes gives you opportunities to help. Boys and girls may have completely different reactions to a book like *There's a Girl in My Hammerlock.* Asking questions like "Why do you think Maisie decided to become a wrestler instead of doing something else that girls usually do?" is a way for you to encourage your child to examine, rather than simply accept, the common definitions of what boys and girls can be and do.

During pre-adolescence, when most children's attitudes toward parental authority and family relationships are changing, book-sharing conversations can give both you and your child opportunities to see the other side of the situation.

Eda LeShan's book *When Grown-ups Drive You Crazy* (yes, LeShan has also written a book for parents called *When Your Child Drives You Crazy*) can give you an opportunity to ask questions like "Do I ever make you feel that way about yourself?" Jeri Bradford, a mother who read this book with her daughter, says that family book sharing has helped her better understand her fifth-grader:

> Not only has it helped me to understand her feelings and attitudes, but it has helped me to see myself through other characters in the book. I am asking myself [and my child] "Do I do or say things that make you feel like I'm this green monster over here trying to control your life?"

Although honest answers to such questions may not always be comforting for parents, such questions and answers can help to build bridges of understanding between parents and children at a time when communication tends to become increasingly difficult.

Reading books like *The Westing Game* can give you and your child chances to have fun with her developing analytical and problem solving skills. Predicting what will happen next or gathering clues in order to make a guess about who is responsible for the crime can be lots of fun. When you use prediction questions with your child, make a special effort to avoid creating a situation that makes your child feel she is being tested. Offer your own predictions as a way of showing your whole-hearted participation. Then you can see whether either of you came close to the actual result.

Reading and Sharing with Kids Ages Twelve to Fourteen

Typical Reading Skills

This is a great time for you to help your child develop the habit of life-long reading for pleasure. Children at this stage usually have stamina for silent, independent reading and are able to take on longer books and novels. They read books with the same motivation that we read newspapers: to gain information about the adult world—a world they are beginning to feel themselves part of. They read for vicarious experience and for the opportunity to try on new roles and to see themselves in new and different situations. These kids are capable of digging out the deeper meanings of stories and usually enjoy talking about the underlying significance of themes and symbols.

Reading Strategies

You may find that reading aloud with maturing readers will make your sharing time seem more natural. When you read a story together, it just makes sense to talk about it as you move along. But if you and your child can't get comfortable reading to one another, try another approach. Consider these reading and sharing strategies:

- This is the easiest stage at which to alternate roles as reader and listener and trade off reading chapters or pages of the book aloud to one another. Make sure to encourage your child to interrupt often so that she can ask questions about, or comment on, how the story is developing. Do the same when she reads to you.

- You may want to get duplicate copies of the books you and your child share so that each of you can read independently. Jerry Nugent says this strategy worked best for him and his son Nicholas:

> When Nicholas would bring a book home from school, I'd go to the library to get another copy. We've tried a lot of the suggestions given at family book-sharing meetings. We tried reading separately and that was fine. We tried Nicholas reading a chapter and then me; rotating it back and forth. This worked excellent for us....We've read some books that I had a hard time getting interested in, but because one of us was interested in it, both of us were.

If you make a habit of marking your favorite passages (Post-It Notes™ work perfectly for this) so that you can read them aloud to one another when you come together for your book-sharing conversations, you will still be able to enjoy sharing the best parts of the story with one another.

- During this time when young adolescents are struggling to form a sense of personal identity, discussing young adult literature with grown-ups of both genders can provide them with important guidance and insight. Fathers should make an extra effort to read and discuss books with children at this age.

Conversation Starters

Book-sharing conversations can provide middle-schoolers with the kind of guidance they need to balance their interest in exciting or even dangerous situations with their own lack of life experience. Such conversations are a great opportunity to discuss things like sexual intimacy in a neutral and non-threatening way. Ask questions like, "What do you think made Didi fall in love with Motown?" If you feel comfortable about doing so, you may want to pose more personal questions like "When you fall in love with someone, what do you think it will feel like? How can you let that person know how much you care?"

Conversation Starters for Children Twelve to Fourteen

As you read books like *The Outsiders* or *The Chocolate War* that deal with peer pressure and peer acceptance, you have valuable opportunities to invite your child to talk about his attitude toward cliques, gangs, and groups and to think about what kind of a group he feels comfortable being part of. Questions like "Who in your group or class do you think you are most like?" or "Who do you think has a very different outlook from yours?" will encourage children to see themselves as unique individuals who are part of a larger group. You might ask questions like "Can you think of a time when everybody else's opinion pushed you into doing something you didn't really think was a very good idea?" Or you might say something like, "You know how Jerry was rebelling in the book *The Chocolate War* and defying Brother Leon's authority? It seems to me that rebellion is just a part of growing up, of trying to figure out who you really are. In what ways do you think you are like that? Who or what do you usually feel like rebelling against?"

As adolescents look for a sense of personal identity, they naturally feel that they need to be independent of the restrictions that parents impose on them. One of the hardest pills parents have to swallow is the apparent loss of importance their own values and opinions have in the eyes of their young adolescent children. Book-sharing conversations may be one more occasion for your child to express her growing sense of independence by voicing opinions that may not agree with your own. In fact, as Barbara Putrich and her daughter Gayle have discovered, "agreeing to disagree" can make your conversations much more worthwhile for both of you:

> We talked about "having our own opinions" before we started family book sharing at home. We talked about how we wanted this to work and how both of us were entitled to express our own opinions. We agreed that agreeing to disagree, or even agree, was okay—I didn't want this sharing to turn into something that would be negative. We talked about how having our own opinion doesn't mean one of us is right and the other one is wrong. It only means that we have an opinion and neither of us expects the other person to change that opinion. We enjoyed this sharing, but I think the big carry-

over was the exposure to each other that we had. We both had this experience of accepting someone else's view—that someone being a person you care very deeply about.

Active Listening Can Start a Chain Reaction

Parents who use the active listening techniques outlined at the beginning of this chapter frequently discover that book-sharing questions will start a chain reaction which leads their children to discuss other, sometimes more meaningful, issues. You can use situations in the books to approach touchy subjects. One mother, Trudy Jester, points this out when she says

> While [my daughter] Becky and I have been doing this program, we have tried to accomplish being more honest with each other. I think honesty is so important during this time for Becky . . . . and I say things to her that probably surprise her. I feel more comfortable saying these things during our book conversations, whereas before, I was at a loss as to how to bring up these topics. Now we talk more about our feelings and we ask each other a lot more about what the other is thinking and feeling.

For her part, Becky says that she feels more secure knowing that her mother is there and will talk honestly with her. As this mother and daughter can verify, parents who practice active listening often get more than just the story the author of a book has written down. The next chapters will show you how you and your child can use writing, art, and drama to share your reactions to books you have both read together.

Bridges to Cross

Talking to your children about their feelings or about the characters in a book demands the same sensitivity that you would use in conversing with any friend: you try to express your opinions without creating a negative impression. Here are some guidelines for friendly book-sharing conversations:

Negative		Positive
• You listen. I'll read.	VS.	Let's take turns reading.
• Listen carefully for details.	VS.	Interrupt at any time.
• Stop whining. Read that chapter to me.	VS.	Let's read first and then talk about the parts we really like.
• When did the boy escape?	VS.	What do you think of the boy's escape?
• Anyone who would act like that is mean and wicked. How can you like him?	VS.	I think that character is really evil. What is it about him that you find interesting?

We want to be active listeners who feel free to express our opinions, to make our own decisions, and to agree or disagree. Our goal, of course, is to end each of these conversations with an enhanced feeling of closeness and respect for one another.

CHAPTER VIII

USING WRITING
TO SHARE IDEAS

> We usually read on our own and then talk
> about the book. We have a dialogue journal
> and I always write to my mom in it. I'm always
> asking her, "How are you doing?" This has been
> fun to do.

Becky Jester, a seventh-grader

Many children and adults feel constrained when someone asks them to talk about their feelings, yet the same people
can write about deep emotions in open and frank terms. Even
when a child knows that others will read his account, he lets
his joys and fears spill out without the embarrassment that
would inhibit him in a conversation about the same feelings.
After she and her daughter read a story about a girl who
brought food to hungry children, Ann Futton asked her seven-
year-old daughter Evelyn if she would write about a hero that
she knew. Here is what Evelyn wrote:

Evelyn

My Hero

I have a hero and he is very very bright and he is nice and he helps Holly when she is in trouble his name is Dennis and he helps other girls thats why every buddy likes him and he likes us.

Evelyn's written statement let Ms. Futton know for the first time that her daughter observed and appreciated the helpfulness and kindness of a boy in her class. Books often bring feelings like these to the surface. Writing about these feelings provides a way for young readers to work through inner struggles. Aswan, a sixth-grader, wrote the following entry in her diary after she had read Judy Blume's novel *Are You There God, It's Me, Margaret:*

WHAT I'M WRITING ABOUT IS HOW I'M NOT ALWAYS SURE OF HOW TO ACT, WHAT TO SAY, WHAT TO DO, OR HOW TO THINK. SOMETIMES, SAYING THE WRONG THING (OR SOMETHING THAT OTHER THINK TO BE THE WRONG THING) CAN BRING UP A LOT OF PROBLEMS. FOR EXAMPLE, IF I WROTE ABOUT DEATH IN A WAY THAT YOU FOUND UNACCEPTABLE, YOU MIGHT THINK THAT I WAS HOMICIDAL OR SUICIDAL. (I'M NOT EITHER OF THEM. IT WAS JUST AN EXAMPLE)

WITH ADULTS, (IF YOU AREN'T AN ADULT) A PERSON IS SUPPOSED TO BE POLITE, THINK BEFORE YOU SPEAK, AND USE GOOD MANNERS. SOME ADULTS APPRECIATE THE CURTESY BUT OTHERS THINK THAT YOU ARE ACTING SNOBBISH OR PHONY.

WITH FRIENDS, OR PEOPLE THAT YOU WOULD LIKE TO BE FRIENDS WITH, WHAT YOU SAY MAKES A DIFFERENCE, TOO. (ESPECIALLY IF YOU ARE AT A NEW SCHOOL). SOMETIMES, WHEN YOU ARE FRIENDS WITH PEOPLE IN TWO DIFFERENT GROUPS, YOU HAVE TO ACT DIFFERENTLY TO BE ACCEPTED.

Aswan's response to Judy Blume's novel opened the door for her and her father to have a conversation about her feelings of insecurity, and for her father to share his own experiences of being unsure of how to act when he was a young adolescent. Books that we think of as good ones usually stir up our emotions, bring to mind old memories, or spark an interesting line of creative thinking for us. Enjoyable books are ones that arouse our hopes, our fears, and our enthusiasm for discovery. Sometimes it will be easier, or maybe simply more fun, for you and your child to share these kinds of reactions by writing about them, expressing them with artwork, or acting them out. As Aswan's journal entry shows, this indirect approach can be a good way to start a conversation about something that one or both of you finds difficult to bring up. It can also be a way for you and your child to add spice and variation to your book-sharing sessions.

As you read this and the next two chapters, you will discover ways you can use writing, art, and drama to share books with your child. Using these strategies will

- help you tailor your book sharing to your child's particular talents and abilities.
- sharpen your child's critical thinking skills.
- emphasize important connections between reading and writing.
- make book sharing more fun.
- help your child see reading as something that is meaningful to her.

When children express their reactions to books in writing or through art or by dramatizing part of a story they are more likely to see books and reading as an enjoyable and real part of their own lives.

Keeping a Journal

When a story arouses feelings or memories from deep within us, writing can be a way of expressing and exploring those feelings. An incident or a character in a story might prompt a child (or an adult) to write about a time when she was feeling left out, hurt, sad, particularly happy, or especially proud of herself. Doing this in a personal journal or diary can be a way for kids to express and thus better understand these feelings. A journal may be entirely private, or each of you may share those passages that you think will keep your conversation moving. Some parents have found that by folding a page over, they can mark and thus keep private those pages they or their children do not want to share.

Expressive writing can be a great way for young people to find imaginative outlets for emotions that may be denied expression elsewhere. It is especially important that parents with children in middle school and high school—the turbulent years—use literature and creative writing to help their teens work through encounters with budding relationships, peer pressure, or anxiety about their future as adults. We've already mentioned that reading gives young people a good channel for dealing with intimacy and the other problems they must face. Writing can be an even better mode of exploration for kids of this age. Sometimes this writing takes on the nature of self-talk, as in this journal entry written by a fourteen-year-old:

My mother says I'm too young to date. I can understand her reasons, since I'm only fourteen. I have a boyfriend, I think I'm in love. My mother doesn't like me to get seriously involved in a relationship this young. I think she's too late. She knew my father when she was my age. They married six years later, divorced 14 [years] after that. My sister is twenty now. She also dated a guy for six years and married him. She's 8 months pregnant.

I'm not saying I'm going to marry my boyfriend. If I do it won't be until after college. I'm not going to plan out my entire life right now. Who's to say how we'll turn out.

For right now, I love him. I guess we'll wait a few years until my mother lets me date. It sure is hard though. I see him at school and he comes over but it's not the same.

In my opinion, I should be able to have a boyfriend without everyone telling me I'm too young to get so serious. I'm not stupid and I'm not going to let anything happen. What is everyone so afraid of?

Encourage your young teen to keep a diary or to write letters, poems, and stories that help him examine his innermost feelings. As one educational expert has pointed out, "It is more important for adolescents to write something than it is for them to write something important." Any form of writing that is supported by constructive feedback from you and respect for your teen's individual privacy can be beneficial to him or her. You may even find that providing a nurturing environment in which your teenaged child can vent deeply felt emotions in print will help to ease family tensions and will actually improve relations between you and your teenager.

Keeping a Dialogue Journal

In a dialogue journal, two or more people take turns talking to one another in writing. Writing in a dialogue journal is a way of sharing important feelings, ideas, and experiences with another person. One father who had started a dialogue journal with his son discovered how writing can provide a valuable outlet for powerful memories and emotions. This father read the book *The Land I Lost* with his son. The book, which is about a boy growing up in Vietnam, brought up memories of the father's tour of duty with the U.S. Army in Vietnam during the war. This man had never talked about those experiences before, either to his wife or to his children, but they became part of the written conversations he had with his son in their dialogue journal. Needless to say, their dialogue-journal exchange added more depth and a whole new dimension to this father's and son's relationship.

Starting a Dialogue Journal

You can start such a journal in an old notebook or writing tablet that you leave in a special place where each of you can make frequent entries. Keeping a dialogue journal is just a way for two people to hold a conversation on paper. Any child who has begun to grasp the basic principles of reading and writing can use this technique. When a parent keeps a dialogue journal with a child who is just learning to read and write, that parent helps her child see how genuinely useful reading and writing actually can be. A parent who starts a dialogue journal with an older child has opened one more important channel of communication with that child.

When children use writing to gain information, imagine stories, express their feelings, or persuade others to accept their opinions, they are writing to achieve a purpose. Printing messages to their moms or dads helps kids learn how to use written language to express their own meanings—it allows them to play with writing and see how to use it to communicate messages that are important to them. Even kindergartners can take advantage of opportunities to explore reading and writing in this meaningful and low-pressure way.

Let your child know that this is not a homework situation, but an opportunity to communicate with you by using writing. Since this is writing intended only as a conversation, a communication of ideas and feelings, it should not be viewed as a homework project that must be edited and corrected. Just go with the flow.

In the following dialogue journal entries, eight-year-old Emily and her mother casually discuss a book about a collie that they have been reading.

Emily,

Are you still reading Beautiful Joe? What is happening in the story?

Mom

> Mom,
>
> i'm Reading Beautiful Joe all Right its great i'm Reading About Mrs. Wood's chikins.
>
> Emily.

Emily—

Tell me about Mrs. Wood's chickens. Is beautiful Joe chasing them or are they chasing him?

Mom

Mom i' Havent finneshr the chapter yet Sri dont No. Emily

Emily,

Have you finished the chapter about Mrs. Wood's chickens? What did they do?

Mom

> Mom,
>
> yes I finished my chappter. I'm on MR.H, MR.A.
>
> I going to tell you aBout the chikens Now
> MRS. Wood came erLey to fead them and they
> thought that they were Late.
>
> Emily.

As he writes to you in your dialogue journal, encourage your child to spell words as they sound—to invent spellings for words he wants to use but isn't sure how to spell. This will allow him to play with language and to "talk" more freely in the journal. Young children can figure out the relationships between sounds and letters, and they can use this knowledge to express their ideas and feelings in writing. For instance, a young child might spell the word "truck" as "chruck" because that's the way it sounds to him. Children will usually start spelling by giving the initial consonant only. Later, as they become more accustomed to writing, they will combine the final consonant with the first one (i.e., "b" and then "bl" for "ball").

Studies show that as children develop, they will add vowels to the consonants so that their words begin to resemble more predictable patterns. Don't let your child's insistence that he is a "bad speller" keep you from sharing in a journal. If your dialogue partner is an especially creative speller, you can make sure each of you understands the other's written message by reading your entries out loud to one another.

Right now you are probably wondering how your child will ever learn to spell properly if you encourage her to invent spellings. She will learn to spell correctly over time as schoolwork and other, more public, writing demand it. You can give her some direction by quietly and patiently modelling the correct spelling for words she spells creatively. To do this, you merely need to rephrase or repeat your child's statements as you add something of your own to them. Notice how Emily's mother makes a point of repeating some of the words her child has spelled inventively in their written conversation about Beautiful Joe chasing the "chikins."

Writing Activities

- ***Have a conversation on paper.*** You and your child can use your dialogue journal to keep in touch about your reading when you don't have time to sit down and read or talk together about books. But your dialogue journal doesn't have to be just for written conversations about books. The two of you can also write messages to one another about other things you want to share.

If you leave the journal in a place where both of you have easy access to it, you and your child can make comments to each other whenever an idea strikes you. For instance, if your child gets home from school while you are still at work, you might greet him with a few comments you've left in your journal. Isn't that a powerful way for you to let him know how much you care about him and to remind him that you're always thinking about him? You will be surprised how just writing notes to one another in an old notebook can add another rich dimension to your book sharing and to your overall relationship. Give it a try and see what interesting conversations the two of you can get going in your journal.

In order to start a conversation on paper, you will need to make the first entry; otherwise your child will probably respond to your invitation with a statement like, "I don't know what to write about." You can begin the conversation by writing a comment about a character or situation in a book the two of you are sharing. Close your entry by writing, "What do you think of this?" or "What were your reactions to this situation in the book?" You can encourage your child to elaborate on his previous entries by making comments like these: "I'm a little confused. Explain to me why Anderson has two homes" or "I'm really curious about Patch. Tell me more about him" or "Don't you think Gillie is a funny name for a girl? How did she get that name?"

Older children might enjoy responding to more complicated questions. You can also use your dialogue journal to do one of the following activities.

- ***Rewrite a story's ending.*** After you and your child have finished reading a story, you might begin a dialogue journal entry with a "What if?" statement. For instance, if you and your child were reading the book *Sarah Plain and Tall,* your child might be intrigued by this question: "What if Sarah had decided to go back to Maine? How do you think the story would have ended then?" Then go on to ask your child to imagine and write his own ending for the book. Encourage him to include as many details as seem appropriate to his age and interest in the story.

- ***Two heads are better than one.*** Use your dialogue journal to write a story with your child. Here's how: one of you writes a sentence or two of the story and then the other one takes a turn with it. You might begin by writing, "Once upon a time there was..." Here's a story eight-year-old Emily and her mother took turns writing:

THE UNICORN

Once upon a time there was a beautiful...
> ...UNICORN NAMED REBECCA, AND SHE WAS SO
> BEAUTIFUL THAT HER HORN AND HER HEELS
> WERE GOLDEN.

She lived in an enchanted woods, where...
> ...ALL THE UNICORNS PLAY. BUT SHE WAS SAD
> BECAUSE SHE HAD NO WINGS TO FLY WITH.

And so many of the other unicorns teased her...
> ...BUT ALL OF THE OTHER UNICORNS WERE NOT
> AS BEAUTIFUL AS HER, AND SO SHE DECIDED TO
> MAKE A PAIR OF WINGS.

Every day for many moons Rebecca gathered
golden pieces of straw...
> ...TO MAKE WINGS WITH. BUT THE OTHER UNI-
> CORNS DID NOT THINK SHE COULD DO IT, SO
> THEY LAUGHED AT HER.

She did not give up, though; she kept working,
and one night when the moon was full she...
> ...REALIZED SHE HAD GROWN BEAUTIFUL WINGS,
> SO SHE DID NOT NEED THE STRAW.

Rebecca said, "What shall I do with all of this
straw?"
> AND SUDDENLY FROM THE GROVE OF TULIP
> TREES SHE SAW A...

...fairy who said to her, "Let me take the straw, please, and I will weave it into a golden castle for you to live in because...

...YOU WORKED SO HARD TO MAKE WINGS AND NEVER GAVE UP.

Besides, I love you, and I want you to live happily forever...

...AND THE OTHER UNICORNS DIDN'T TEASE REBECCA EVER AGAIN, AND THEY WISHED THEY WERE AS BEAUTIFUL AND THEY HAD A CASTLE, TOO.

THE END

- *Write your own sequel.* Have you ever had the experience of enjoying a book so much that you hated to see it end? One solution to that problem is to write your own sequel. Marge Simic's twelve-year-old son Bobby thinks this is a terrific way to keep a good story alive. He loves creating new problems for his favorite characters to solve. When Bobby had read his way through all of the books in the *Encyclopedia Brown* series, he decided to write his own *Encyclopedia Brown* mystery. Bobby thinks writing sequels is so much fun that he's begun to write another one. This one is a follow-up to *Alice In Wonderland.* Here are the first few paragraphs:

WONDERLAND MAGIC

It was a lazy day at Alice's house. She was playing with her cat Dinah. What she needed was a friend. She was bored with playing with a cat, she wanted a human friend.

"Oh Dinah," said Alice, "I don't want to be rude, but you're boring. I can't have a good conversation with you."

Dinah meowed.

"See, it's hopeless," sighed Alice.

Alice got up from her chair and walked to the window. She pulled back the drapes and saw some children playing hide-and-seek. She thought to herself, "I'll go outside and play with them." She opened the door. Dinah got up from the chair and followed Alice.

Alice and Dinah walked out the door. Suddenly a huge dog chased Alice and Dinah through Alice's house. The dog trampled over Alice to get to Dinah. Alice fell to the floor. Dinah jumped up on the mantelpiece and went through the magical looking glass. The dog, a little confused and a little scared, ran away. Alice got up and said, "Oh Dinah, wait for me!" She climbed up on the mantelpiece and went through the looking glass. Alice found herself in a dark forest with brightly colored trees. Then she heard some voices....

(Bobby's imaginative sequel to *Alice in Wonderland* is continued in Appendix A at the back of this book.)

Here's another sequel in which a young writer draws more directly from her everyday experience. After reading one of the *Sweet Valley High* Books, Rhonda, a middle-school student, wrote this story in her journal:

JONATHON
AND
TAMINA

JON AND TAMINA ARE GIRLFRIEND AND BOYFRIENDS. JON IS THIRTEEN AND SO IS TAMINA. THEY BOTH GO TO MYRTLE AVENUE SCHOOL. JON HAS TWO FRIENDS, THEY ARE VERY CLOSE. THEY GIVE EACH OTHER ADVICE. TAMINA HAS TWO FRIENDS, SHE LISTEN TO OUR ADVICE WHEN SHE NEEDS IT. JON AND TAMINA LIKE EACH OTHER VERY MUCH THEY HAVE STRONG FEELINGS FOR EACH OTHER....THERE RELATIONSHIP IS VERY GOOD BUT THEY PLAY TOO MANY GAME. THEY BROKE UP ABOUT THREE TIMES ALREADY AND THEYVE GONE BACT TOGETHER IT'S STUPID. THE LAST TIME THEY BROKE UP SHE GOT MAD, ALMOST CRIED AND HE DID THE SAME THING. IT SEEM LIKE THEY CANT LIVE WITHOUT EACH OTHER.

Even young children can create short sequels to stories they enjoy. Invite your child to imagine her own story with her favorite characters in starring roles. She can dictate her story to you as you write it down. If your child wants to illustrate her story, you can make a book of it by fastening the pages together with brads or staples or by sewing them with strong thread. Protecting the covers of your child's book with clear contact paper will make it sturdier and better able to survive numerous readings.

Books for Young Writers

Books can serve as great writing models for children, especially when those books portray characters who use writing in fun and meaningful ways. Here's a list of books which do just that:

- *The Jolly Postman, or Other People's Letters* and *The Jolly Christmas Postman* by Janet and Allan Ahlberg (letters between folktale characters; for kids ages four and up). As the postman pedals his way through this book, he makes deliveries to young readers as well as to the characters in the stories. The pages are creatively designed as envelopes that children can open to find letters from folktale characters. The book offers an excellent introduction to writing: the envelopes contain letters, postcards, occupant junk mail, and even book-club offerings.

- *Dear Annie* by Judith Caseley (letters between a girl and her grandfather; for kids ages four to nine). This book features some of the letters exchanged between Annie, her mother, and her grandfather from the time she is a baby to the time when she shares all of the letters with her grade-school class during show-and-tell.

- *George Shrinks* by William Joyce (letter; for kids ages six to nine). This picture book is a letter from George's parents telling him what chores he should do while they are out.

- *Stringbean's Trip to the Shining Sea* by Vera B. Williams (story in postcard form; for kids ages six and up). This story is told through the postcards that Stringbean sends to his family in Kansas to tell them about his trip to the shining sea.

- *Onion Tears* by Diana Kidd (story partially revealed in letters; for kids ages eight to eleven). A Vietnamese girl comes to terms with the trauma of escaping from her country without knowing what has happened to the rest of her family.

- *Anastasia Krupnik* by Lois Lowry (Anastasia makes lists and writes poems; for kids ages eight to eleven). In this book, the first of a series, Anastasia is the only girl in fourth grade whose name will not fit on the front of a sweatshirt; the teacher doesn't like Anastasia's attempt at free verse; and Anastasia is sure she is going to hate the arrival of the new baby. Each succeeding novel in the Anastasia series chronicles some new quandary.

- *My Side of the Mountain* by Jean George (diary; for kids ages ten to fourteen). A modern-day Robinson Crusoe, city-bred Sam Gribley describes his year surviving as a runaway in a remote area of the Catskill Mountains. His journal account of living off the land includes moving stories about the animals, insects, plants, people, and books that helped him survive.

- *Hey World, Here I Am!* by Jean Little (poems and journal entries from Kate; for kids ages ten to fourteen). Kate uses her journal to talk about the difficulties of friendship and to continue her search for her own identity. In this book, the third in a series, Kate expresses her thoughts and feelings in poetry and prose.

- *A Gathering of Days: A New England Girl's Journal* by Joan Blos (historical fiction in journal entries; for kids ages eleven and up). A fugitive slave whom Catherine never meets brings changes to her life.

- *The Burning Questions of Bingo Brown* by Betsy Byars (journal entries full of interesting questions; for kids ages eleven to fourteen). Bingo uses his journal to agonize over such profound questions as how much mousse his hair needs, which of three girls he should pay attention to in his sixth-grade class, and how he can get one of these girls to hold hands with him.

- *Dear Mr. Henshaw* by Beverly Cleary (story told in letters and journal entries; for kids ages eleven to fourteen). Using only the letters and diary of a young boy named Leigh Botts, Cleary traces his personal growth from first to sixth grade. This diary allows the reader to watch the changes in Leigh's relationship with his divorced parents, see him in a succession of new schools where he always ends up the friendless new kid, and participate in the relationship that develops between Leigh and an author with whom he corresponds over the years. Most importantly, the book traces Leigh's changing relationship with himself.

- *A Girl From Yamhill: A Memoir* by Beverly Cleary (memoirs from the author; for kids ages eleven and up). Beverly Cleary's memoir speaks to adults who have read her books, as well as to older kids. Glimpses of her popular book characters can be seen in the word portraits Cleary draws in this memoir of people from her own childhood. Among other things, the book reveals the difficult relationship Cleary had with her own mother. This can be a fruitful topic of conversation for parents and teenaged kids.

- *Anne Frank: The Diary of a Young Girl* (historical World War II diary; for kids ages eleven and up). Anne's diary reveals the thoughts of an adolescent growing up under extraordinary conditions. It tells the true story of how Anne and her family hid from the Nazis for two years in the secret annex of an office building in Amsterdam.

- *Germy Blew the Bugle* by Rebecca Jones (articles in a school newspaper; for kids ages ten to fourteen). Jeremy Bluett, who is called "Germy Blew It" by his sixth-grade friends, launches a school newspaper despite unwilling reporters, a principal who refuses to let him sell advertising, and deadline troubles.

- *The China Year* by Emily Neville (letters; for kids ages eleven to fourteen). Fourteen-year-old Henrietta Rich (Henri) spends a year in Beijing while her father is working as a foreign expert at the university. Henri's letters give readers a first-hand view of what it's like to live in a modern Chinese city. The story takes place just before the Chinese army drove into Tienanmen Square.

- *Z for Zachariah* by Robert O'Brien (novel in diary form; for kids ages eleven and up). This science-fiction novel begins during a nuclear war. As Ann hears radio stations go off the air one by one, she believes that she is the last living person on earth. Then she begins to carve out a life alone, accompanied only by the family dog. Ann keeps a diary of what she does to survive and of her growing resolve to find other survivors.

- *Libby on Wednesday* by Zilpha Keatley (creative journal entries; for kids ages eleven and up). Libby is an eleven-year-old who has been home schooled by well-educated adults. When she goes to public school, she is placed in the eighth grade where she wins a writing competition and then becomes part of a five-person writers' group. Libby feels uncomfortable in the group and so retreats to her treehouse where she records insights about her group members' personalities in her journal. Although Libby's journal is a personal one, she ends up sharing it with the others in her group in hopes that it will help them understand one another better.

- *Strider* by Beverly Cleary (journal entries; for kids ages eleven and up). This book is the sequel to *Dear Mr. Henshaw*. The story begins four years later when Leigh is a high-school student and a track runner who still writes in his diary. Leigh befriends an abandoned dog on the beach and it is the dog that helps Leigh get through his father's abandonment and the conflicts created by a love triangle between himself, his only friend, and a girl hurdler.

- *An Owl in the House: A Naturalist's Diary* by Bernd Heinrich and adapted by Alice Calaprice (for kids ages eleven and up). This account studies the life cycle of an owl.

We hope these suggestions will give you and your kids ideas about using writing to vent deeply felt emotions, to share books, and to create your own stories.

CHAPTER IX

USING ART TO SHARE BOOKS

I think one thing that's been interesting about this experience is that you realize how much we depend on TV for entertainment. We forget to listen and use our imaginations. The reading and sharing brought that all back for me.

Bebe Kinnett, a mother

A Picture Can Be Worth a Thousand Words

After you read a book or part of a book, encourage your child to think about it and then draw a sketch (or make a painting, a collage, a mural, or a sculpture) that expresses what the story meant to her or reminded her of. Using art to share books is especially appropriate for younger children, for older children who enjoy creative projects, or for those kids who feel that writing in a dialogue journal is "too much like homework." Drawing can also make the process of learning how to listen more productive for some kids. Mastering the art of listening is not easy. Becoming a good listener is a talent that must be patiently and gradually cultivated. You may find that reluctant readers or unusually active children have a hard time just sitting still and listening while you read. Giving these kids paper and markers or crayons so that they can "draw" the story or express their reactions to it as you read provides them with a way to keep their hands busy while they listen.

Many young children are more confident expressing their reactions to books through artwork than they are talking with you about stories or writing in a dialogue journal. Drawing really is a form of written expression for young children. For them, pictures speak in a special language. Little kids tend to "read" books by looking at the pictures that illustrate the stories. As they begin to decipher print, they use illustrations as clues that direct their guesses about unfamiliar words. Because pictures speak so clearly to these kids, they are usually eager to talk with interested adults about the stories embedded in their own artwork. They like to translate into words the ideas their pictures express in visual images.

Talking with them about what they have made is an important part of sharing with young children. If you listen to your child talk about her drawing, collage, clay sculpture, or painting and then ask questions that invite her to tell you what she was thinking about as she made it, you will send your child a clear and important message: you will let her know that her thoughts and ideas really matter to you. If we just look at our kid's art and offer a few general compliments, we miss much of the value of using this as a way of sharing feelings and ideas. Encourage your child to talk about her artwork. Ask her to talk about how her painting or clay sculpture retells the story or shows a connection between events in the story and her own experiences.

Make a habit of building bridges between pictures and language by offering praise that describes how and why you like certain parts or details. Encourage your child to write or talk about how his artwork illustrates a feeling or idea he got from the story. Sometime this will be as simple as labelling a picture with the name of a place or character.

Some kids just naturally lean toward creative activities and seem to have a talent for art. Parents of such kids get used to having drawing paper everywhere. They are accustomed to seeing clay dinosaurs cavort on the window sills and watching worn-out socks become animated puppets. These parents naturally save bits of yarn, colored paper, bright scraps of fabric, or a bird feather found on an afternoon walk, because they know that their children will turn these things into the stuff of art. If you are the parent of one of these visually creative children, your kid will probably be excited by the prospect of using art to share books with you.

But if your child doesn't think of himself as a good artist, you may need to help him focus on using his drawing or collage to express an interpretation of the story rather than on the brilliance or inadequacy of his artistic talents. A friend of mine who taught art in elementary schools for many years says that she is convinced all children are budding Van Goghs and Matisses until they reach the age of eight or nine. Then, at a certain point in their growing-up process, the majority of children decide they are not "good artists." If your child seems to have made such a decision, encourage her to express her feelings and ideas with art and discourage her inclination to judge her work as "not good enough." You can do this by finding things in her work or in her thought process to praise.

Your willingness to take an active role in using art as a book-sharing activity will probably have a big influence on its success or failure. Even five-year-olds know that sharing is usually a two-way exchange. Use your book-sharing time as an opportunity to jump into an art activity with your kid. Even if neither of you really knows what you're doing, the two of you can have fun figuring it out and making it up as you go along. The activities described in the next section will make it easier for you to do that. Your participation will enable your child to use art and drawing as a way to understand how different people can have different reactions to the same story. Talking about your individual interpretations can be a great way to start a conversation about books.

Setting the Scene

In school, kids are too often given a box of crayons and a small piece of paper and told to draw a picture about a story they have just read or heard. By providing an intriguing collection of "stuff" that can be made into art, you will let your child know that this is not just another school assignment, but an opportunity to have fun with you. Collect chalk, paint, markers, yarn, colored tissue paper, steel wool, tape, cotton balls, fabric scraps, modelling clay, glue—anything that you and your child might use to make an illustration of a story.

You might even want to make a craft cabinet in which your child can store his "art" supplies. One teacher tells me she made such a cabinet by taping together used Pringles cans. As soon as her family emptied a can, she would bring it to school where her students would tape it into the already existing collection. Each can was a little cubby hole, and the whole collection was a great way to organize markers, glue, fabric scraps, tape. If you want to make a craft cupboard that has larger cubby holes, you might try taping, pasting, or stapling six or eight old shoe boxes together. In this mini-display case your child can store the small treasures he will use to create impressions or tell stories.

Once you have interesting materials and a place to keep them, you can further encourage your child to use her artistic imagination by asking the kinds of questions that will help her think about how she can use her artwork to communicate ideas about stories. Questions like the following ones will help kids (and adults) think through and plan their book-sharing art projects:

- What materials do you think we should use for our picture?

- What colors does this story make you think of? Where should we put those colors in our picture?

- What characters should we include? How should we make these characters look? What will they wear? What kind of look do you think this character should have on her face?

- What is special about this character or scene that makes you want to include him or it in our painting?

- How did you make that part of your picture? Tell me what you were thinking about when you painted, drew, or added this?

- Will you tell me the story as your pictures show it?

Both children and adults may need several opportunities to try using art as a way of sharing before they gather enough confidence to play with the meanings they are discovering through drawing or assembling found materials into a visual pattern. But don't give up on this strategy for sharing. It can be an especially rewarding one. Give some of the following activities a try.

Art Activities

- ***Create a Rorschach (blotter) painting.*** Do you remember seeing old movies in which a psychiatrist shows his patient a symmetrical inkblot and then the patient unwittingly reveals his innermost thoughts when he describes what the inkblot looks like to him? Those abstract designs formed by the inkblot can give rise to surprising revelations and interpretations. Here's an example of a blotter print I made with my three-year-old niece, Hannah. When Hannah looked at the painting she had so carefully created, it looked sort of scary to her. Since the most frightening character she had recently encountered was the Big Bad Wolf (we had just finished reading *Little Red Riding Hood*), Hannah decided she had created a portrait of that fairy-tale villain.

The Big Bad Wolf

Art Activities

You and your child can also create colorful inkblot paintings at home—and use them to spark fascinating conversations about books you read together. Making blotter paintings is easy and fun to do. This way of painting is so rewarding partly because every try yields a strikingly beautiful product. And it's an artistic endeavor that is as enjoyable and appropriate for three-year-olds as it is for young teens. Here's how to do it.

All you need are spoons, at least two colors of liquid paint (using red, yellow, and blue will give you the most interesting mix of colors), and some paper.

1. Begin by folding the paper in half; then open it up.

2. Use the spoons to drop very small amounts of paint on the paper. Be careful to keep most of the paint near the center of the paper.

3. Fold the paper in half again and gently rub the paint around.

4. Open the paper and see your beautiful painting.

5. Talk about what the painting reminds you of and give it a title.

One mother who has done family book sharing with her kids says that she frames her children's paintings and gives them as gifts. Her friends and relatives are charmed by her kids' work and the kids themselves find it a real ego boost to see their creations hanging up in someone else's house.

- *Make a collage about a book.* You don't always have to make a drawing or a painting to use art to share books with your child. In fact, assembling found materials into a collage may be an easier project than drawing or painting a picture. All you will need is some cardboard on which to assemble your collage, a bit of glue, and a willingness to use your imaginations. Use anything from common natural artifacts like pine cones and acorns to pictures and photographs cut out of magazines as materials for your collage. You will probably be surprised by the kinds of materials you can use to reflect your reactions to a book or to retell a story.

- *Draw or paint a mural and use it to decorate a wall in your house.* Murals make great collaborative art projects. All you need to create one is a theme, some paint or markers, and a big sheet of butcher paper or newsprint. You can use a book you are reading together as your theme. You will probably have to spend some time talking together to plan your mural before you begin drawing it. You might organize your mural around the events in a story or around a combination of your child's favorite story characters. Instead of drawing the images on the mural itself, you may want to make smaller drawings that you can cut out and paste onto the larger mural. Then you can draw or paint around them and watch the mural take shape over time.

- *Create a story museum.* This activity is especially appropriate for older children. You and your child can create a "museum" collection of artifacts that remind you of characters, symbols, objects, themes in books you have read together. Museums are just labelled collections of objects. You and your child can have fun making a museum that contains a collection of objects that represents a story (or a group of stories) that you have read together. Your display cases will be sheets of paper or cardboard on which you draw your collection.

Art Activities

Your museum can illustrate or say something about a story or a group of stories you have read together. Label and explain the significance of each item in your collection and you will have a personal archive of objects from all the books you have read together.

- ***Create a comic strip with characters from your favorite books.*** If your kid takes a liking to a particular character, you and she might make that character the star of your own comic strip. A mother who read the *Ramona* books with her kids told us that her son had so much fun with this fictional character that he created a comic strip with Ramona as the star.

Art Activities

You and your kids can start a family comic strip by taking turns drawing and writing captions for different frames of the strip. If you want some tips about how to draw cartoons, check out the following books:

✍ *Ed Emberly's Great Thumbprint Drawing Book*

✍ *Ed Emberly's Drawing Book: Make a World*

✍ *Ed Emberly's Drawing Book of Faces*

✍ *Ed Emberly's Drawing Book of Animals*

Emberly's books (which are most appropriate for kids ages five to ten) give easy, step-by-step instructions for drawing animals, people, and objects. Children will be delighted by their ability to draw using these simple combinations of lines and geometric shapes.

The following books feature step-by-step directions that will enable older children (ages eleven to fourteen) to draw cartoon figures from basic shapes:

✍ *The Art of Cartooning* by Syd Hoff

✍ *Draw 50 Monsters, Creeps, Superheroes, Demons, Dragons, Nerds, Dirts, Ghouls, Giants, Vampires, Zombies, and Other Curiosa* by Lee Ames

• **Create a book quilt with scraps of fabric and permanent magic marker.** You and your child can create an heirloom out of your book-sharing experience. All you will need is a bed sheet and some indelible magic markers or fabric paint. Cut the sheet into 12-inch squares. When you read a story together, talk about what characters or scenes your child liked and then ask him to draw a picture about them on one of the fabric squares. If you do this for each story or book you read together, you will soon have enough squares to piece together into a quilt. If you are not handy with a sewing machine, perhaps someone else in your family will be able to assemble the quilt. The craft and needlework section of your local library will probably have books with instructions about how to make simple quilts and comforters.

- **Build a diorama.** A diorama is a three-dimensional scene. Using cardboard boxes or shoeboxes, kids can recreate and interpret one of their favorite scenes from a book. Help your child gather real objects and create or sculpt figures for your diorama. You may need to return to the book you are illustrating to check descriptions and facts. Making a diorama is a fun project for parents to do with older children.

- **Write and illustrate your own books.** You might choose to collaborate with your child on a project like this by agreeing that one of you will write the text of the book and the other one will make the illustrations. Browsing the library book shelves for books that have won Caldecott Awards will give you imaginative ideas for illustrations, styles, and use of various media. Caldecott Medals are awarded to books that have distinctive and especially creative illustrations.

Books for Young Artists

- *Straight Is a Line: A Book About Lines* by Sharon Lerner (for kids ages three to five). Brief text and bold graphics illustrate lines that are straight, parallel, vertical, and horizontal, as well as lines that curve and zigzag. Children can match the lines shown with lines they see all around them.

- *I Want a Blue Banana!* by Joyce and James Dunbar (for kids ages three to five). Dan accompanies his mother to the grocery store. While she is looking for her lost list in the produce section, he learns the names of several colors and fruits.

- *Gerald-Not-Practical* by Helena Clare Pittman (for kids ages six to nine). Gerald loves to draw, but his family wishes he would do something more practical. Gerald eventually teaches his family that drawing makes him happy. He shows them how important it is to do something you truly love. This book supports children who enjoy art more than other activities.

- *Bonjour, Mr. Satie* by Tomie de Paola (for kids ages six to nine). When Pablo and Henri present their new paintings at Gertrude's salon, terrible arguments begin. Mr. Satie, a traveling cat, is chosen to judge whose paintings are the best. All of Paris awaits Mr. Satie's decision.

- *Cherries and Cherry Pits* by Vera B. Williams (for kids ages six to nine). Bidemmi draws lots of pictures, and with each picture she tells a story while she draws. This book demonstrates the creative outlet art provides for children and shows the value of a good imagination.

- *The Young Artist* by Thomas Locker (for kids ages eight to eleven). Young artist Adrian Van Der Weld faces the dilemma of painting the king's courtiers as they want to look, not as they appear. Even though it is difficult and dangerous, Adrian maintains his sense of integrity and receives his just reward.

- *Da Vinci. Picasso. Rembrandt. Van Gogh.* Written by author/illustrator Mike Venezia (for kids ages seven to twelve), each of these four books tells children about the life of a famous artist. Venezia's humorous text and illustrations invite children to look at the world of art in a fun way and to see famous artists as real people.

- *The Collage Book* by Hannah Tofts (for kids ages eight to eleven). This book explains what a collage is and gives simple instructions about how to make one. It presents examples of collages made from paper, fabric, wood, food, photos, and other objects.

- *Rembrandt's Beret* by Johnny Alcorn (for kids ages eight to eleven). Tiberius becomes lost while waiting for a rainstorm to end and discovers the "Hall of the Old Masters." Mysteriously, he meets the artists. As a result of their meeting, Rembrandt honors Tiberius by painting a portrait of him.

- *The Eleventh Hour: A Curious Mystery* by Graem Base (for kids ten to fourteen). This sophisticated picture book for older kids requires readers to play detective. They must use visual and verbal clues to solve a riddle. The answer to the riddle is revealed in a sealed "Inside Story" section at the end of the book.

- *Black and White* by David Macaulay (for kids ages ten to fourteen). This book's outstanding illustrations and intriguing text may tell several different stories that do not necessarily occur at the same time. On the other hand, there may be only four different stories or a single story told in four parts. Readers must carefully evaluate both words and pictures in order to decide.

- *From the Mixed up Files of Mrs. Basil E. Frankweiler* by E. L. Konigsburg (for kids ages eleven to fourteen). Claudia wants to teach her parents a lesson in "Claudia appreciation" and so decides to run away from home. She plans to live in comfort at the Metropolitan Museum of Art and invites her little brother Jamie to go too, mostly because he is a miser and will have money. When the two of them take up residence in the museum, they are confronted by a fascinating mystery.

Let your imaginations lead you into new and interesting ways of sharing your feelings and ideas with one another. We hope the books and activities suggested here will give you and your child a place from which to start.

CHAPTER X

USING DRAMA TO SHARE BOOKS

My younger sister doesn't like to read, but she does like comic books. Veronica from the *Archie* comic books is her most favorite character. Sometimes when my mom and I are reading, I hear Dad reading to her in the other room, and he's so funny because he pretends to be Veronica. Lindsey just loves it.

Leslie Bradford, a fifth-grader

Making Stories Come to Life

If you have ever read a bedtime story to a toddler, you know how changing your voice to fit the dialogue can delight your reader and make the story come alive in new ways. Dramatic reading can have a similar effect on older children. You may think the idea of an adolescent sitting with his parents for a reading session sounds ridiculous. But watching these "macho" figures sit spellbound as a reader who is willing to put some drama into her voice causes the exploits of a great hero to come alive, or makes gory descriptions of mayhem seem truly horrible, can be inspiring. All you have to do to make stories come alive for your listeners is to pick the right book and read it with enthusiasm. You only have to be willing to ham it up a little bit.

Gayle and Barbara Putrich have discovered how much fun hamming it up really can be. They say that they like to "choose parts" and read their characters' words in dramatic voices. Gayle and her mother, Barbara, see this as a fun way to inject "something different" into their book-sharing time. It helps them become more emotionally involved with the story because they say they tend to identify with a character whose part they act out. Here are a few general hints about how you can use drama to make your read-aloud sessions more fun:

- ***Reading too fast is a common mistake for readers of all ages.*** Getting into a character's mind is one way to ensure you will read slowly enough for your readers to build vivid mental impressions of people and places.

- ***Adjust your pace to fit the different parts of the story.*** For instance, slowing down and drawing your words out during a suspenseful part of the story and speeding up when the action gets fast and furious will inevitably bring your readers to the edges of their seats.

- ***Lead by example.*** If you are not afraid to ham it up a bit, your children will probably be more willing to make a story come to life by taking on the part of one of their favorite characters.

Drama Activities

If you think you and your child might enjoy using drama as a way of sharing books, give one of the following activities a try.

- ***Make your own living room or kitchen into a* Reader's Theater.** *Reader's Theater* involves reading a story aloud and basically acting out the different parts with your voice. It is an oral interpretation of the story and characters that requires neither costumes nor movement. There's also no memorization of lines because all the lines are in the story you are reading together. The focus is on the story, not on the actors. Only facial expressions, tone of voice, and maybe a few gestures are important in *Reader's Theater.*

  Stories with a lot of dialogue work best for *Reader's Theater.* Readers choose the character or characters whose dialogue they want to read in the story. Even young readers will be able to recognize the dialogue spoken by their character or characters when you point out that those words, phrases, or sentences appear in quotation marks. The person who is taking the part of the narrator reads the parts of the story that describe scenes, events, situations, or themes—that is, the parts of the story that do not appear in quotation marks.

  You can make a *Reader's Theater* happen in your own living room, in your kitchen, or in your kid's bedroom. The place is not important; it's your rendition of story that matters. This is a great activity to share with the rest of your family. They can take a part or be the audience for the "performance." Audiences clap, you know. You may want to encourage your child to practice or read over his part before you use your voices to act it out for your audience. Practicing for *Reader's Theater* allows both proficient and less accomplished readers to be successful in reading aloud.

- **_Listen to a talking book._** Talking books can be valuable tools for making children's literature come alive. At the same time, they also provide good models for expressive oral reading. Most libraries have collections of books on tape for young, adolescent, and adult readers. Children and adults can listen together to a story being read on cassette while they follow along in their copy of the book. Listening and following along in the book focuses on interpretation and allows the reader/listener to become involved in the story. Listening to talking books is a fun way for children to enrich their vocabularies and increase their word recognition.

- **_Create your own talking book, or better yet, encourage your child to make one._** Taping books written for young children is easy—they don't take a lot of time and you can put several books on one tape. Young children who get into the habit of hearing their favorite books read in an animated and expressive way will most likely become animated and expressive readers themselves.

  When my own four children were young, I read to them nightly, even into their middle-grade years. But often my work took me out of town, and so I had to invent a way to continue bedtime reading. I gave my children a sense of my presence by tape recording a new installment of our bedtime reading. Thus they could listen to our continuing story and go to sleep just as if I were actually present.

  If your child is a reluctant reader who resists reading aloud with you, you may find that taping the first few chapters of a book is a good way to get her "hooked" on a story's plot. Once your child gets into the book by listening to those few chapters, she will continue reading on her own. If you stop taping at an especially exciting point in the book, you will give her an added incentive to pick up where you left off.

Perhaps an older child would enjoy creating talking books for a younger family member, an older relative, or just for you. Tell her to see the tape recorder as an appreciative audience and to read each part with dramatic expression. Taped books can make great gifts for grandparents or for aunts and uncles. Think how proud your child will be to hear his relatives praise his taped reading.

- ***Act out your favorite stories in a puppet theater.*** You can use finger puppets, shadow puppets, or puppets created from old socks or paper bags to dramatize stories. To make finger puppets, you only need to draw faces on your own and your children's fingers. Or if you want a more sophisticated finger puppet, you can tape to your fingers cardboard faces on which you or your child has drawn eyes, nose, mouth, and hair. Then move your fingers as you speak in the character's voice. You will be surprised at how easily young children get caught up in and identify with puppet characters.

To create a shadow puppet theater you will need construction paper or tagboard, scissors, a stapler or tape, long straws or tongue depressors, and a lamp. Make your shadow puppet by drawing and then cutting out the silhouette of one of your child's favorite characters such as Curious George, Frog or Toad, or Amelia Bedelia. Then staple or tape the puppet onto a long straw or tongue depressor. Make a blank wall into your shadow puppet stage by taking the shade off a lamp that has a bright bulb in it and then using the light to cast the shadow of your puppet on the wall. Make several characters to star in your play.

You can make hand puppets out of any number of easy-to-find materials. You and your child can make a very simple hand puppet by using a Ping-Pong ball for a head and a plain handkerchief for the body. The puppeteer puts the handkerchief on her index finger and then inserts her finger in a hole in the ball. If you use two rubber bands to secure the handkerchief to thumb and forefinger, you can create arms for your puppet. Old socks also make great hand puppets, as do small paper bags. Magic markers can be used to draw on facial features and yarn threaded through a big needle can be sewn on to create hair or fur. Children can make sock hand puppets appear to talk by moving their fingers and thumb.

Create a stage for your hand or finger puppets by sitting or kneeling behind a tabletop. Another simple stage can be created by hanging curtains so that they cover the upper and lower parts of a doorway or by placing a turned-over table or a cardboard box positioned on its side in the doorway. Making your stage in a doorway has the added advantage that children who are waiting their turns offstage are hidden from view. Puppet shows are a good way to get the whole family involved.

Books for Young Actors

- *The Napping House* by Audrey Wood (for kids ages three to five). This clever story is set in a cozy bed on which a snoring granny, a dreaming child, a dozing dog, and a horde of other characters all end up sleeping at the same time. Daybreak brings a surprise ending. The story is presented in a series of rhymes, each of which repeats and extends the ones before it (like "Old MacDonald" or "The Farmer in the Dell"). Encourage children to recall the sequence of the sleeping characters as they appear in this story and to act out with play what each character does in the story.

- *Finger Rhymes and Hand Rhymes* by Marc Brown (for kids ages three to five). These two books give children clear directions for using finger and hand gestures to act out short poems. Children may learn and play rhymes such as "Where Is Thumbkin?" or "Five Little Goblins" or "Here Is the Church."

- *The Three Billy Goats Gruff* by Peter Christian Asbjornsen and Jorgen E. Moe (for kids ages three to five). This favorite folktale for young children is about three goats who "trip-trapped" across the troll's bridge to eat the green grass on the other side. The story uses vocabulary and word patterns that children can easily put to motions and sounds. Repeated phrases, fast action, and an economy of words encourage children to participate in this story by using dramatic play or hand puppets.

- *Amazing Grace* by Mary Hoffman (for kids ages six to nine). Grace wants to try out for the part of Peter Pan at school, but her classmates tell her she can't since she is a girl and she is black. With the help of her family, Grace discovers she can be anything she wants to be. Because she has the courage to speak up and try out, Grace gets the part and gives an excellent performance.

- *Strega Nona* by Tomie de Paola (for kids ages three to seven). Strega Nona owns a magic cooking pot that may be started by saying "Bubble, bubble, pasta pot" to make all the pasta anyone needs. But Big Anthony, a true noodlehead, starts the pot without observing Strega Nona's method of getting it to stop: blowing three kisses. Children will enjoy chanting Strega Nona's magic words.

- *Frog and Toad* series by Arnold Lobel (for kids ages five to seven). Discussion of whose house they will go to is just one of the many conversations in this series about Frog and Toad. These easy-reading books full of dialogues between Frog and Toad are an excellent series for trying *Readers' Theater* with young children.

- *Little Red Riding Hood* by Trina Schart Hyman (for kids ages three to seven). This familiar children's folktale encourages children to chime in and play-act the adventures of Little Red Riding Hood and the Big Bad Wolf. Parents and children can use *Readers' Theater* with the dialogue in the story.

- *Mother Goose, A Treasury of Best Loved Rhymes* by Watty Piper (for kids ages three to seven). Of the many nursery rhyme books available today, this volume is an excellent choice for extended use with children. It has a good collection of familiar rhymes, large illustrations, bright colors, and, it's not too heavy to handle.

Encourage children to learn the rhymes and rhythms that accompany Mother Goose rhymes.

- *Sing a Song of Popcorn* by Beatrice Schenk de Regniers (for kids ages three to seven). What distinguishes this volume from other excellent poetry collections is that each of the nine sections has been assigned to a different Caldecott Award-winning illustrator. These include Maurice Sendak, Trina Schart Hyman, and Arnold Lobel. The sounds and sights of this book are outstanding. Encourage children to use their bodies to act out these lively poems.

- *Shadow Play* by Paul Fleischman (for kids ages six to eleven). This book shows how a man in a circus sideshow dramatizes the story of "Beauty and the Beast" with shadow puppets. Readers get an inside view of how the puppeteer creates his drama when the children in the circus audience go backstage after the performance.

- *The Magic School Bus* series by Joanna Cole (for kids ages six to nine). This science series is one of the most popular and innovative informational picture books of recent years. Science information is packaged in humorous asides and funny conversation balloons that parents and children can easily turn into *Readers' Theater.* Children embark on field trips in the Magic School Bus and learn about the human body, a waterworks station, the solar system, and the earth. All of these fantastic field trips are presided over by Ms. Frizzle, a memorable teacher. Children will love taking part in Ms. Frizzle's expeditions with her class.

Books for Young Actors

- *The Master Puppeteer* by Haru Wells (for kids ages twelve to fourteen). This novel is set in eighteenth-century Japan. It tells the story of how Jiro, the son of a starving puppetmaker, runs away from home to apprentice himself to the ill-tempered master of a famous Japanese puppet theater.

- *The Tales of Uncle Remus: The Adventures of Brer Rabbit* by Julius Lester (for kids ages eight to eleven). This collection is a more rambunctious version of the usual African-American folktales about Brer Rabbit. Parents and children can have fun with the dialect these talking-critter tales offer.

- *When the Sky Is Like Lace* by Elinor Lander Horwitz (for kids ages eight to nine). Learn how to prepare for a "bimulous" night, when the sky is like lace—when otters sing, snails sulk, and trees dance. Discover which foods to eat, what color to wear, and with whom to talk. This is a great book for doing *Readers' Theater.*

- *Heroes and Monsters of Greek Myth* by Bernard Evslin (for kids ages eleven to fourteen). This collection of Greek myths uses modern vocabulary that makes the stories seem more contemporary, so it is a great way for parents to introduce children to Greek mythology. These contemporary retellings of ancient myths that are designed to appeal to children lend themselves easily to dramatization. You can dramatize them as straightforward *Reader's Theater* or add some extra spice by pretending they are heroic, old-timey radio plays.

- *The Great Gillie Hopkins* by Katherine Paterson (for kids ages twelve to fourteen). When Gillie arrives at her next foster home, she can't bear her new foster mother. Gillie learns to accept and give love for the first time in Maime Trotter's home. The first chapter of *The Great Gillie Hopkins*, where Gillie is being driven to her fourth foster home by the social worker, makes a wonderful scene to use for trying *Readers' Theater* with adolescent children.

- *Joyful Noise* by Paul Fleischman (for kids ages ten to fourteen). Older children particularly enjoy practicing reading these poems for two voices. All these poems are about insects.

- *Roll of Thunder, Hear My Cry* by Mildred Taylor (for kids ages ten to fourteen) is the story of the Logan family, their pride in the land they have owned since Reconstruction, and their determination not to let injustice go unchallenged. The dialogue in this story lends itself well to *Readers' Theater.*

The Active Reader

The past three chapters have highlighted ways to make stories and your conversations come alive through writing, art, and drama. These are just resources to which you can turn when you and your child want to try something different during your reading and sharing time. Certainly, they are not intended as ways to test your expertise as a writer, artist, or actor, but as ways for you and your child to have fun and talk with each other. Enjoy! Praise! Encourage! Be natural!

Chapter XI

BUILDING SELF-ESTEEM

One student commented that she was really impressed that her parents took the time to share with her. This child knew that Mom and Dad were real busy, and yet they would find the time to sit down and talk about a book with her. That made the child feel real important.

—*Darla Staley*
middle-school teacher

My class evaluation shows that I am improving. I'm going up in my vocabulary and getting a little better in comprehension. That makes me feel good.

—*Kentowan Marshall*
middle-school student

The Failure Cycle

Many kids are unable to separate "I'm not very good at reading or math" from "I'm not very good." Low self-esteem hinders children's school performance, and poor performance in school leads to poor self-esteem. When a child feels this way, he gets caught up in a cycle of academic failure that is like a merry-go-round from which he has more and more

I'm Not Very Good

trouble jumping off as time passes. Low self-esteem leads to failure and each failure further undermines his self-esteem. Thus, the kid gets caught up in a continuing pattern of failure and bad feelings about himself.

Children often get special instruction in those subjects that make them feel like they are "not very good," but we parents need to work especially hard to help them develop their sense of self- respect.

Some psychologists go so far as to say that maintaining or increasing our current levels of self-respect is the prime motivator of all human behavior. A person with a high level of self-esteem will tend to act in ways that reinforce his self-image. A person who sees himself as a failure will expect to fail and will set himself up to act in ways that are consistent with his self-image. If a child thinks he is a winner, he will behave like a winner. But if a child thinks he is a loser, his behavior will reflect that belief.

Although this may sound simplistic, psychiatrists are generally in agreement that each of us thinks of herself as either a success or a failure. One feeling tends to overwhelm the other until we have either a success feeling or a failure feeling about ourselves. You can consciously use family book-sharing strategies to influence your child's image of herself as a winner. Conversations about books can provide opportunities for you to say to your child: "Your ideas are valued. You are growing into a good person. You can always talk to me about your beliefs and your feelings."

Did you know that a child's level of self-esteem can be a more influential factor in her academic success or failure than her level of intelligence is? Researchers have shown this surprising fact to be true. They developed tests that assess children's level of self-esteem and then administered these tests to a group of children who were just entering school. Thirty months or so later, the researchers evaluated these children's reading skills and achievement scores. The children who had the highest levels of self-esteem in kindergarten also had the highest reading scores two and a half years later.

As a result of these tests, the state of California (for one) has revised its educational goals. The revised goals designate increasing children's sense of self-esteem as one of the major aims of education. California teachers distinguished this as the fourth most important goal of education and placed it right behind reading, writing, and arithmetic.

Self-Esteem Is a Feeling

A child's sense of self-esteem is a collection of feelings. It's a combination of how a child feels about herself and how she perceives that others feel about her. Self-esteem forms an important part of a child's self-image. Whereas self-esteem or self-respect is a feeling, our self-image is a set of ideas or beliefs we have about who we are. Self-image can be reported. Each of us makes statements about what we like or don't like, about what roles we think we play in relation to others, about what values we hold. However, we usually tend to act out rather than talk about our levels of self-esteem.

A child with high self-esteem tends to

- express pride in his own accomplishments: "Look at this! Don't you like the drawing I just made?"
- enjoy independence and attempt to do things on her own: "I made my own lunch today."

- assume responsibility easily: "Sure, I'll sweep the floor for you."

- be able to deal with frustration: "This puzzle sure is hard to put together, but I'll bet I can figure it out."

- approach new challenges with enthusiasm: "Wow, the teacher said that we are going to start learning how to write in cursive tomorrow!"

- feel that she is capable of influencing others: "Are you proud of me when I bring home A's in reading?"

- express a varied range of emotions and feelings: "I feel happy when Dad's at home, and I miss him when he's gone."

A child with low self-esteem tends to...

- belittle her own talents: "Nothing I draw looks any good."

- express a sense of powerlessness: "I can't find my reading book. Where's the paper? I lost my pencil. I'll never get my homework done!"

- be easily influenced by others: "Everybody else was doing it, so I did, too."

- avoid situations that involve the possibility of failure: "I am not going to go to school today. There's a hard test in science."

- feel that others don't value him: "I don't have any friends. No one likes to play with me."

- make others responsible for her own failures: "You didn't help me study for my spelling test. That's why I got a bad grade on it."

- exhibit an inability to deal with frustration: "It's not my fault that I can't figure out how to put this dumb model together. I'm just going to smash it."
- express a narrow range of emotions: "I don't care if Joanna doesn't want to be my friend. I never really liked her anyway."

A child who acts in several of the ways described above, and who does so consistently, has probably been unable to develop a healthy level of self-esteem.

A child's sense of self-esteem is so important because it influences all of his relationships. This includes the extremely powerful relationship a child has with himself. Loving and caring for others is an impossibility without self-love. A child is able to respect others only to the extent he is also able to respect himself.

The Four Conditions of Self-Esteem

Child-development experts tend to agree that most children form their self-images between the ages of five and ten. After that it is difficult, although not impossible, to change the picture a child has of herself. Every child has the potential to develop a strong self-image and a high level of self-esteem. In this way, children are like plants who flourish when they get all of the nutrients, water, and sunlight they need. For children's sense of self-esteem to grow and flourish, certain conditions must also be met, and you may be surprised to notice that none of them has anything to do with money or material wealth.

1. In order to develop high self-esteem, a child needs a firm sense of belonging.

Feeling like he is an important member of a family, class, gang, team, or ethnic group helps a child build a strong self-image. Feeling "part of something," feeling related to other people in significant ways, means that a child can share his feelings and ideas and be assured that those who care about him will pay attention to him. This means letting your kid know that his statements and opinions are heard, considered, and respected. A kid's need for a sense of belonging also extends to connections back in time and space. Have you ever noticed how enchanted your children are by family stories about the past and by your memories of them as babies? Share those memories often.

2. In order to develop high self-esteem, a child needs to feel unique.

A child gains a lot of self-esteem from feeling that she is part of a group, but at the same time it is essential that children develop a firm sense of their own individuality. Children with high self-esteem generally get lots of support and approval for being special or standing on their own two feet. Every child needs to be encouraged to express herself in her own way. You can encourage your child to enjoy being different by continually letting her know that she has unique talents and that she can do things no one else can do. Most children's need to establish a sense of their own uniqueness is so strong that if their virtues aren't sufficiently acknowledged by those important to them, they will identify their negative characteristics as those that make them "special."

3. In order to develop high self-esteem, a child needs a sense of power.

Children need to feel that they can exercise influence on people and events in their own lives. In order to develop a healthy self-image, a child must feel he can set goals (even simple ones like picking up his toys or finishing an interesting book) and then follow through and achieve those goals. Fulfilling responsibilities (like studying for a test or finishing household chores) also gives a child a sense that he knows how to be successful. Parents who teach the necessary skills, provide the resources, and praise efforts help their children develop a sense of personal power.

Build your child's self-confidence by letting her make decisions about things that directly affect her (Would you like a peanut butter or a tuna sandwich for lunch?). Learning how to make choices and solve problems enhances kids' sense of independence and personal control. However, forcing children to make decisions about things that are clearly beyond their capacity often has just the opposite effect. Setting limits and clear rules for behavior and requiring children to share in household chores are critical contributions parents can make toward helping their kids develop a real sense of personal power and responsibility.

4. In order to develop high self-esteem, a child needs good models to follow.

Three different kinds of models help children figure out how to behave in and make sense of the world:

a. Human models show children how to act. A child needs adults, teachers, parents, siblings, friends, and fictional heroes whom he can emulate. Children learn best by example; they mimic people around them. The parent who says "Do what I say, not what I do" is ignoring this crucial law of imitation because children will mimic both negative and positive behaviors that they see. For instance a child who never sees her parents pick up a book or magazine will be unlikely to become an avid reader.

b. Philosophical models or standards for behavior also guide kids' actions. Kids who hear and see a consistent set of values (honesty, hard work, cooperation, or lack of respect for school and academic pursuits) practiced in their family tend to adopt those values. Religious values and the values expressed in school also impress the consciousness of children and help to direct their behavior.

c. Past experiences constitute powerful models for a child's behavior because these enable a child to make predictions about the outcomes and consequences of similar future events and behavior. For instance, a child who gets what he wants when he screams learns that screaming is an effective strategy that he can use in the future.

Building Your Child's Self-Esteem

If you flip back to the preface of this book, you will notice that I made a promise to you when you began to read *Connect!* I promised you that this chapter would show you how you can consciously use family book sharing to raise your child's level of self-esteem. Well, here's how.

1. Use family book sharing to strengthen your child's sense of belonging:

- Show affection through physical contact. Touching children is an important way to strengthen their sense of belonging and connectedness. Kathy Buck says this about sharing books with her sixth-grade daughter, Julie:

  > We set aside this half-an-hour to an hour every night and I enjoyed just being close enough to touch Julie, reading the same thing and talking. That sounds so simple, but how many of us really talk to members in our own immediate families? We don't give the important ones in our family enough of that one-on-one time.

- Make eye contact while you share your reactions to books. Eye contact increases intimacy. When people look at us as we talk to them—when they allow their faces to express their feelings and reactions—we are more connected to them.

- Reassure your child of your positive feelings about him. Saying things like "It makes me feel good to talk about this with you" or "I like it when you read to me" lets children know that they please you and that they have the power to make you happy. Affirming statements like these build kids' self-esteem, but they also do something more: they teach your child that making positive statements to others is an important way of establishing connections and intimacy. Thus, such statements improve children's abilities to build positive relationships.

Strengthen Your Child's Sense of Belonging

- Share your own feelings and reactions to books with your child. It's important for children to know that your feelings don't always result from what they do. Sharing some of your own victories and failures with your child can make you seem more human, and thus a more realistic model of adult experience. Likewise, choosing to read books that give you a chance to talk about your own interests, hobbies, and memories will further build and strengthen your child's connections with you. Involve your children in what you do and talk to them about how the activity makes you feel and about why you do it.

- Take this opportunity to listen to what your child has to say without judging his statements and opinions. Listening in this way is an art, and it is an important way to respond to your child. You can practice this art (and in the process, build your child's self-esteem up a notch or two) just by being quiet and letting your child talk, especially if you encourage him to talk to you about himself. Don't feel that you have to comment or advise or make suggestions every time he says something. Ask broad questions (rather than specific ones that might seem like prying or that will bend the conversation more in your direction) and practice active listening by rephrasing his statements so that he will elaborate on and extend them.

- Invite the rest of your family to be part of your book sharing. Bebe Kinnett says this has been a real benefit for her family:

  > J.R [a twelve-year-old] and I started to read and then Sean [ten-year-old] said he wanted to listen. And Neil [five-year-old] didn't want to be

left out so he joined us, too. I don't think Neil understands everything. He usually only lasts ten or fifteen minutes to half-an-hour and then he falls asleep. But he still comes back the next night and wants to listen even though he might miss half of the story the night before. I don't think he cares if he gets caught up with the book or that he gets bits and pieces of the story. Neil considers it a family thing. He is part of the family and he just wants to be there with us.

2. Use family book sharing to nurture your child's sense of her own uniqueness:

- Encourage your child to express ideas that are different from your own. Agree to disagree. If a child is ever going to develop good problem-solving abilities, he must feel secure in pursuing his own train of thought. Book-sharing conversations are a great place to practice this skill.

- Point out that you appreciate your child's special way of doing things. Talking about how her reaction or approach to a problem would be different from that of a character in a book will let your child know you are aware of her unique qualities. You can also encourage your child's individualism by allowing her to complete assigned tasks or chores in her own way. Giving children approval for doing a job (organizing their toys, cleaning up the yard, deciding how to decorate their rooms) in a unique way raises their own sense of individuality and self-esteem.

- Increase your child's opportunities to express himself creatively. Children with low levels of self-esteem tend to limit their own imaginations. The stories they tell and the pictures they draw tend to be dull and ordinary. Because such children are uncomfortable with change, they usually engage in repetitive play and mimic what others do. This is true partly because kids with little appreciation of their own uniqueness can't muster much confidence in their own ideas. Try using creative writing, art, or drama activities to share books with your child. Praising his written or visual creations and appreciating his dramatic interpretations of stories is one more way you can encourage your child to gain confidence in his own ideas.

- Allow your child to pursue an interest that has grabbed her fancy. Don't be concerned if your child seems to develop "obsessions" that endure for a while and then give way to another interest. Children's interests change over time, and temporarily immersing herself in one activity can be just another way for your child to express her individuality. When this happens, go to the library and help your child choose books that reflect her current passion. By doing so, you invite your child to share her interests with you.

3. Enhance your child's sense of power:

- Help him become aware of how he makes choices and decisions. The ability to make choices comfortably gives one a sense of personal power. Kids make choices all of the time, but they are usually unaware of how they arrive at those choices (by weighing alternatives, predicting consequences, making decisions based on values). You can use conversations about the actions of a book character to discuss the decision-making process and to talk about how we all make decisions about how to act. Choosing books together offers you and your child a good opportunity to discuss the decision-making process.

- Use book-sharing conversations to name and explore feelings. Children often blame other people, events, or even fate for the way they feel. Learning to take responsibility for and understand our feelings is part of growing up—for most of us it is a lifelong process. Children who feel powerless tend to consistently blame others for the way they feel. Talking with your child about his reactions to a story in a way that encourages him to name and explore his own emotions can make a child feel he has more control over himself and hence over his own life. Using the creative book-sharing strategies mentioned in Chapters VII through X may facilitate these kinds of discussions.

- Allow children to think through and to solve their own problems. In their desire to protect their children, parents often give their children too much help solving problems. Children's sense of self-esteem and personal power rises dramatically when they realize that they have thought through a knotty problem by themselves—even if the solution isn't perfect. All good stories center on a conflict or a problem that must be resolved. Encourage your child to predict what he thinks will happen in a story once the central problem has been presented. Predicting what will happen can be a good way for your child to hone his critical-thinking abilities.

- Encourage your kid to try new activities and accept new challenges. One boy who took part in family book sharing, was very pleased by his ability to accept the challenge of reading a "big 700 page novel." Proving himself equal to this task gave J.R. a new sense of self-confidence and personal power. Books that touch on new and perhaps frightening experiences can help kids accept new challenges.

- Read books that undermine gender stereotypes. This is especially important for girl children. Studies show that boys and girls generally have similar levels of self-esteem until they reach the age of nine or ten when they become more curious about gender roles and gender differences. At this point, little girls often suffer a marked loss of self-esteem. Perhaps that is because the traditionally feminine gender-role tends to curtail little girls' opportunities for self-expression and other challenging activities. Studies have shown that adolescent girls who seem androgynous or masculine tend to have higher levels of self-esteem than those adolescent girls who adopt what are traditionally considered feminine traits and behavior. Book-sharing conversations can be a great opportunity to broaden your child's understanding of what it means to grow up male or female.

4. Provide your child with strong models to emulate:

- Point to the wide world of information and varied experience books can provide. Children often use past experience to predict the outcome of events and behavior. Stories in books can provide another sort of experience for them to rely upon and can give them new information about their world.

- Use situations in books to clarify values and beliefs. Helping a child talk about beliefs clarifies them and makes those guides for behavior more usable for her. Thirteen-year-old Becky Jester points this out when she says

  > My mom and I get along but it's different now. We really sit down and talk about some really important things about growing up and other life situations.... [I] know what she likes and what she expects of me. We talk about drinking and all that. She lays it out pretty clear when we talk, but I know the choices and decisions will be my responsibility.

- Show your child that reading is important. Telling your child to develop good reading skills will not encourage him to benefit from the rich pleasure books can bring to his life. However, actively reading and discussing books with him will provide him with a persuasive model to follow.

Reassurance

I am sure you will find that setting aside special time to read and talk about books with your son or daughter will make a real difference in your child's level of self-esteem. For your part, don't be surprised if family book sharing ends up giving you a special boost of parental self-respect. It might even make a difference in your own attitude toward books and reading. Deborah Bova, a junior-high-school teacher in Indianapolis, Indiana, describes how family book sharing changed one mother's approach to reading:

It's not just kids that are benefitting from this program. I mentioned that we have a parent who told me that she didn't read very well. I encouraged her to stay in the [family book-sharing] group because I told her that the way a person learns to read is by reading....I helped her select books I thought she could read and that would hold her interest. She has come to every meeting and she said "I just can't get over how I like these [books]. I'm able to read them." She started out with books that were probably at a fourth-grade level. I'd say she's up to about sixth or seventh grade at this point. That's a wonderful accomplishment....Her daughter is really pleased with her mother, too. Her daughter said to me, "You know, my mom reads more books. She's read more books than she's ever read. I just think that's great!"

CHAPTER XII

JUST DO IT!

A sneakers company ended one of its commercials with the challenge: Just do it! That challenge could easily be your slogan as you finish this book. If you find yourself intrigued by some of the thoughts and some of the people who spoke to you in these pages, why don't you try those ideas in your family? The benefits to you and your children are numerous, so why not follow the guidelines found here and begin. Just do it!

If you still wonder about the power of reading books and discussing them with your children, you may want to read the final report of the *Parents Sharing Books* Project, 1993 (available from the Family Literacy Center at Indiana University). That report covers in detail how to gather together families who want to learn how to read and to talk about books of mutual interest. The final report of the project describes the operation and the people who participated. Their stories and their numbers are given in detail.

The *Parents Sharing Books* Project had the twofold purpose of promoting family reading and improving family communication. It succeeded in both purposes, but the favorite topic of conversation among the parents and children who participated was their improved communication. It surprised the hundreds of participants how much their family relationships improved as a result of this one simple vehicle—sharing ideas about the same book. To be honest, it amazed us on the project team as well.

The first *Parents Sharing Books* Project, which was supported by the Lilly Endowment, Inc., of Indianapolis, helped hundreds of families and middle-grade schools. The project functioned in inner cities, suburbs, small towns, and rural areas. Our first priority was to draw in families and schools in areas that have a high percentage of poverty. The concept worked with those schools and also with other parents who were not restricted by low incomes. What pleased us about the wide variety of successes we found was that the book-sharing concept worked in all kinds of school and family settings. Low-income families and high-income families found equal benefit in the family communication that resulted from using books as a starting point.

Guidelines for Action

What we have learned from the project, however, can benefit you as you think about talking with your children. Several important guidelines arose from the work that we all did together:

1. All kids want their parents and grandparents to pay attention to them. When you offer to read one of their books or magazines "Just so I can talk to you," you show your kids that you want to know more about them as people.

2. To talk comfortably, parent and child need a common interest. A novel or a short story give you an immediate common interest. The story line forms your interest—you don't have to fake interest in some current childhood fad.

3. You can read aloud to kids of all ages. One way to get started is simply to read a few pages to your child. "What do you think of the way this story begins?" High-school kids seem to enjoy listening to stories as much as younger kids.

4. Initially ask your child to choose the book that you both will read. Later you may want to use other guidelines, but at first you want to make sure that your child has a book or a topic that will appeal to him. Most parents find that they actually enjoy the books their children choose.

5. Show respect for the ideas and opinions of your child. Without a doubt, that means listen to your child and respond positively to some aspect of what she says. Communication will cease in a hurry if the child feels that most of her ideas are being rejected or ridiculed. You may certainly express your own opinions, but your purpose here is not to win arguments; it is to hear and understand the ideas of your child.

6. Express your own ideas as opinions, not as laws. Since your discussion starts with incidents in a book, you can say: "In my opinion, he acted inappropriately." Your child may disagree with your opinion, but the playing field for the two of you allows equal time for opinions about what is happening in the book.

7. Build an atmosphere for sharing ideas. Outside of reading a book together, ask for your child's opinion on all kinds of things that go on in the country, in the neighborhood, in the home. "What would you do about that if you were principal of the school?" And try to learn why your child gives the opinion that he does.

8. Make time. Find time. Your child will recognize your effort to find a few minutes for her several times a week. She will respect the effort you made to put her in an important place in your life, a time when you shared ideas together.

9. Invest in yourself. Besides the books you read with your children, read to make you a better person, a better parent, a better worker. Listen to audio-tapes or watch videotapes or attend workshops that will build your knowledge and your skills.

10. Get help from local resources. Form a mutual help group. Librarians, teachers, bookshop personnel, counselors, and church leaders are all at your service. Talk to them and ask for ideas and for guidance. You may find all the help you need in a group of parents who, like you, want to improve family communication and are willing to form a mutual help group.

Maybe you have already taken the first step and begun to read and share books with your kids. If you have, you know that maintaining your commitment to family book sharing is going to take some determination. Most of us find that our determination is bolstered by those friends and family members who take the time to listen to us talk about our current struggles and then offer an encouraging word. You probably will find it easier to make reading a family habit if there are some other adults with whom you can compare notes and share your experiences. One way to start a mutual support group is to pass this book along to a friend or a neighbor whose family might also be interested in reading and sharing books.

There is, however, a more reliable way for you to enlist the kind of support that will help you get book sharing to really work in your family. If you think you would find sharing your experiences with other parents to be motivational, I strongly encourage you to start the wheels moving toward getting a family book club started in your community. Consider recruiting the aid of

- your child's teacher.
- your child's Boy Scout or Girl Scout troop leader.
- the religious education director at a local church.
- an active member of a single parents' support group.
- PTA/O volunteers.
- the children's librarian at your local library.

By lending this book to one or two of the people listed above you can pique their interest in the idea, but you might also find that a more detailed plan would be an advantage. The Family Literacy Center at Indiana University has developed a training manual entitled *Parents Sharing Books* (PSB) which is designed to provide book-club leaders with all the information and materials they need to set up a book club and lead a series of book club meetings. These informal gatherings can provide valuable interaction for children as well as for parents.

Barbara Putrich says that these meetings served as a real incentive for her daughter to continue with family book sharing:

> I noticed Gayle coming home after our PSB meetings and telling me about books that we just had to read. The kids that came to our meetings would sit off in their group and talk about the books they were reading with their parents or on their own...I think the interaction that these kids were having during PSB was great. It provided incentive to continue reading. It wasn't just parents saying "Let's read this." Everybody was in the act—teachers, parents and kids—suggesting books to read.

Family book sharing really encourages everybody to get in on the act because it builds bridges of communication between parents and children, between home and school. And there really is something in it for everybody. It's surprising that such a simple idea can have such powerful effects. Give it a try and see for yourself.

References

Atwell, N. *In the Middle: Writing, Reading and Learning with Adolescents.* Portsmouth, NH: Boynton/Cook-Heinemann, 1987.

Bean, Reynolds and Harris Clemes. *Raising Children's Self-Esteem: A Handbook for Parents.* Capitola, CA: APOD Publications, 1978. ED 176 867.

Bode, Barbara. "Dialogue Journals: A Different Kind of Talking Book." *Parents and Children Together: Teamwork Learning 3.5,* Nov. 1992. 15-21.

Donelson, Kenneth and Alleen Pace Nilsen. *Literature for Today's Young Adults,* third ed. New York: HarperCollins, 1989.

Faber, Adele and Elaine Mazlish. *How to Talk So Kids Will Listen & Listen So Kids Will Talk.* New York: Avon, 1982.

Fahey, Mary. Your Child's Self Esteem, a Family Affair (Unit for Child Studies Selected Papers Number 7). Kensington, Australia: New South Whales University Unit for Child Studies, 1980. ED 204 035.

Hart-Hewins and Jan Wells. *Real Books for Reading: Learning to Read with Children's Literature.* Markham Ontario: Pembroke, 1990.

Huck, Charlotte S., et al. *Children's Literature in the Elementary School,* fifth ed. Ft. Worth: Harcourt Brace Jovanovich College Publishers, 1993.

Kobin, Beverly. *Eyeopeners! How to Choose Children's Books About Real People, Places and Things.* New York: Penguin, 1988.

Maron, Chris. *Children's Feelings About Themselves* (Unit for Child Studies Selected Papers Number 1). Kensington, Australia: New South Whales University Unit for Child Studies, 1980. ED 204 029.

Marshall, H. H. "Research in Review: The Development of Self-Concept." *Young Children,* 44.5, 1989. 44-51.

Mernit, Susan. "Kids Today." *Instructor,* September 1990, 35-43.

Mullins, Ronald L. and Kathleen Mckinley. "Relations Between Adolescent Gender Role Orientation, Self-Esteem and Social Conformity." Paper presented at the Annual Conference of the National Council on Family Relations (49th, Atlanta GA, November 14-19, 1987).

National Center for Education Statistics, U.S. Department of Education. *Statistics in Brief: Home Activities of 3- to 8-Year-Olds.* Washington D.C.: Government Printing Office, 1992.

Raines, Shirley and Robert Canaday. *Story S-T-R-E-T-C-H-E-R-S for Primary Grades.* Mt. Ranier MD: Gryphon House, 1992.

Teale, W. "Parents Reading to Their Children: What We Know and Need to Know." *Language Arts,* 58, 1981.

Trelease, Jim. *The Read-Aloud Handbook.* New York: Penguin, 1987.

Appendix A

WONDERLAND MAGIC
BY BOBBY SIMIC

Draft # 1

It was a lazy day at Alice's house. She was playing with her cat Dinah. What she needed was a friend. She was bored with playing with a cat, she wanted a human friend. "Oh Dinah," said Alice. "I don't want to be rude, but you're boring. I can't have a good conversation with you." Dinah meowed. "See, it's hopeless," sighed Alice.

Alice got up from her chair and walked to the window. She pulled back the drapes and saw some children playing hide-n-seek. She thought to herself, "I'll go outside and play with them." She opened the door. Dinah got up from the chair and followed Alice.

Alice and Dinah walked out the door. Suddenly, a huge dog chased Alice and Dinah through Alice's house. The dog trampled over Alice to get to Dinah. Alice fell to the floor. Dinah jumped up on the· mantlepiece and went through the magical looking glass. The dog, a little confused and a little scared, ran away. Alice got up and said, "Oh Dinah, wait for me." She climbed up on the mantelpiece and went through the looking glass. Alice found herself in a dark forest with brightly colored trees. Then she heard some voices. Are you sure that's the same cat that beat you at croquet?" said the voice.

"Of course it is. Would you doubt the queen?" said the other voice.

"Sorry, your Majesty," said the voice.

"Now then, shall we go through the short cut," said the other voice.

"Yes, your Majesty," said the other voice.

"The cat shall be beheaded at 12:00 this morning."

"Twelve o'clock," thought Alice. "Isn't that a little late? But this time is looking glass time. Everything's backward. Oh, I hope it's not Dinah's who's in trouble, but how could she get in trouble? She just got here. Well, I better follow them. If I only knew where the shortcut was.

Alice traveled on the path through the woods. Then she saw a sign. It said: Tulgy Wood. "I wonder what's in Tulgy Wood. It certainly sounds curious." Alice walked a little farther until she heard a voice humming. Then a smiling cat appeared up in a tree. "Why it's a chesire cat," Alice exclaimed.

"Where?" said the cat.

"You," said Alice.

"Me?" asked the cat.

"Yes," said Alice.

"Who?" asked the cat.

"Never mind," said Alice. "Can you tell me a shortcut through this woods?"

"What woods?" asked the cat.

"This woods," said Alice.

"Oh, Tulgy Woods," said the cat.

"Yes," said Alice.

"What?" said the cat.

"What a strange cat," thought Alice.

"Do you know where the un-birthday party is for the Queen of Hearts?" asked the cat.

"I don't know, but you could come with me and we could find it together," replied Alice.

Well, okay," answered the cat. Alice and the chesire cat traveled down the path. They saw a tall hedge of bushes. Alice was tall enough to see over. She saw a huge table of tea pots, cups, and saucers. There was a man with a large hat and a hare with a suit and tie on. They seemed to be sad. Alice thought she might cheer them up. She told the cat her idea. They went through the gate and went to the table.

"What is wrong?" asked Alice.

"It's the Dormouse's birthday," sobbed the hare.

"What's wrong with birthdays? I happen to like them," replied Alice.

"Don't you see?" said the man with the large hat. "A birthday is the only time of the year that you don't get presents."

"I get presents on my birthday. Another thing is that I don't see a mouse anywhere."

"He's in there," pointed the hare to a teapot in the middle of the table.

Alice opened the lid of the teapot. The Mad Hatter leaped from his chair and landed on Alice's head, "Don't disturb him. This is a sad day in his life. Try to be kind to him," said the Mad Hatter.

"You are rude," added the March Hare, "walking in on his sad day like this."

"Well," Alice said pulling the Mad Hatter off her head. "If you don't want me here then I'll take the chesire cat and go."

"What cat?" asked the March Hare.

"He couldn't have just disappeared," said Alice.

"A chesire cat can," said the Mad Hatter.

"Oh no," sighed Alice as she left. Alice's stomach growled. "That's strange. I just ate, but I don't know how long I've been gone. I probably missed tea."

Alice traveled down the path. She seemed to be going down a hill. When she got to the bottom of the hill, she saw a sign that said: "Brumpy Valley." "I wonder what a Brumpy is," thought Alice. "Alice noticed that there were little houses and that she was taller than the houses. Each house had a garden in the back with tiny little vegetables. "I am hungry," said Alice. "Maybe I could have just a little taste. "If they do come out, I'll be bigger than them. I'll just fight them off. They're probably as big as dollhouse dolls. Why I have dollhouses bigger than their homes."

Alice went to a garden and pulled up a carrot. She took a little bite. Suddenly, Alice started shrinking rapidly. Alice screamed. The houses felt normal to her now. Alice knocked at one of the doors. Nobody answered. Alice opened the door and went in. The inside of the house was just like Alice's. Even a miniature Dinah was there, even though it wasn't miniature to Alice.

Alice went to a chair and sat down. Dinah jumped on her lap. Alice thought to herself, "I wonder if the outside of the house is like mine. I didn't really look carefully."

Alice got up from her chair and walked to the front door. She opened it. Alice heard a dog barking. Alice stepped back inside, but she didn't close the door. Then a dog came running in. Alice ran out the back door and lept into a bush. The dog ran right past her. "I better get out of here and get to my right size," thought Alice.

Alice ran down the path and up the hill. Now everything was big to her. She walked off the path and into a flower garden. In the garden was a cocoon. It started to break open. Out came a huge butterfly.

He said, "Whoooo arrre yooou?"

"Why, I'm Alice."

"Never talked to an Alicccce before," said the butterfly sleepily.

"I've never talked to a butterfly," said Alice.

"And a handsome butterfly at that. Look at my colorful wings," said the butterfly.

"Why yes, they are lovely, but do you know a way for me to return to my right size," replied Alice.

"What is wrong with your size?"

"It's dreadfully small and..."

"Why you're the same size as me!" exclaimed the butterfly.

"Nothing's wrong with your size, it's mine."

"Oh, I see, you don't like being my size," said the butterfly.

"Well...."

The butterfly's face turned red. He swooped down aiming for Alice. Alice jumped on a plant's leaf. The butterfly bent back the plant. Alice held tight. The butterfly flung it back and sent Alice flying through the air. Alice soared through the air. She closed her eyes. Then she heard a splash. She was swimming in some red liquid that tasted like cherries. Alice swam up to the top and looked out. Looking over was a rabbit with clothes on and a big fat lady that had hearts all over her clothes.

"There's a bug in my punch," she exclaimed. "Go and kill it right now."

"Yes, your Highness, right away."

"But I'm not a bug. I'm a little girl," said Alice.

"Little! that's right but you're a bug," said the heart lady. "Whoever disagrees with the Queen of Hearts shall be beheaded."

"I know who I am," yelled Alice.

"OFF WITH HER HEAD," screamed the Queen of Hearts.

"Off with her head," yelled the rabbit.

"Wow, two beheadings and an unbirthday party," said the Queen of Hearts.

Alice got picked up by the white rabbit and put in a cage with a certain cat, Dinah!

"Oh Dinah, am I glad to see you!" exclaimed Alice.

"Me too!" replied Dinah.

"Dinah, you can talk," said Alice in surprisement.

Ya, when I went through the looking glass I was able to talk."

"How did you get in this cage?" asked Alice.

"The Queen of Hearts took me as the wrong cat. She thinks I'm the chesire cat."

"You don't look like the chesire cat."

"I know. You know how stubborn she is."

"Yes, now we have to find a way to get out," said Alice. Alice and Dinah thought for awhile. Then Alice thought of something. "If a carrot made me small, I wonder if something could make me big," said Alice to Dinah.

"That might work if we could get some food," added Dinah.

Alice, a little disappointed, thought for some time. She over-heard what the White Rabbit was saying: "Come on you guys work. Get the food for the queen's party Duce," the rabbit said to a card, "get the cake." "We'll have to hurry." Alice had an idea.

"If we asked for food and started to yell then the queen would give us food so we would be quiet so we won't spoil her party," said Alice.

"Good idea," replied Dinah. The two started to yell and scream. The White Rabbit came up to the cage.

"What do you want," he said.

"We're very hungry, Mr. Rabbit. Would you please give us some food," said Alice.

"If you stop yelling I will," he replied.

"We promise," said Dinah.

The rabbit went off and came back with a small glass of tea. "Thank you," Alice said. She took a sip. Suddenly she started to grow. She grew bigger and bigger. She was way past her size, her head hit the ceiling, but she kept growing. Her head went through the roof when she finally stopped.

"Cards!" commanded the Queen of Hearts, "Attack!"

The cards fluttered in Alice's face. If felt like hands were slapping her. The cards grabbed her legs and started shaking her. Suddenly everything around her exploded until there was nothing around her but darkness.

❄ ❄ ❄ ❄ ❄

Alice opened her eyes. A girl was around her. "Wake up," said the girl.

"Where am I?" said Alice getting up.

"My dog trampled you down. You were out for a couple minutes."

"A couple minutes? I've been gone for a day," replied Alice.

"And where have you been?"

"I've been in a wonderland."

"Oh well, I like people with good imaginations. My name's Rachel."

The two girls walked out the door leaving Dinah all alone. Alice finally got a friend.....a human friend.

Index

Resources for Families

Connect! How to Get Your Kids to Talk to You
by Carl B. Smith with Susan Moke and Marjorie R. Simic

This inspiring book shows you how to make book sharing and open communication a reality in your home. **G49; $14.95**

Parents Sharing Books, Technical Report
by Carl B. Smith and Marjorie R. Simic

This report chronicles a three-year program which linked parents, children, and schools through the establishment of mutual help groups. Sample case studies give detailed examples of how to make a book-sharing project work in various school and community settings. **M11; $14.95**

Family Book Sharing, Leader Training Manual

This comprehensive manual enables a local leader to conduct at least six meetings for family members interested in sharing books as a means for increasing reading and communication. Agendas, activities, handouts, resources, letters, press releases, etc., give leaders a ready-to-use package for an entire project. **M03; $85.00**

Video for Parents Sharing Books

Shows various strategies that parents and children use for holding book conversations. Parents and teachers report the significant changes that these strategies have brought to their lives and those of their children. **V01; $24.95**

¡Leamos!/Let's Read!
by Mary & Richard Behm

101 practical ideas, side-by-side in Spanish and English, for parents to help their children develop reading and writing skills at home, at the store, in the car—everywhere! **G45; $8.95**

101 Ideas to Help Your Child Learn to Read and Write
by Mary & Richard Behm

The same great ideas as ¡Leamos!/Let's Read! in English only. **G08; $6.50**

Help Your Child Read and Succeed: A Parents' Guide
by Carl B. Smith

Guidance for beginners and for intermediate readers. Lots of activities to help with comprehension, study, phonics, vocabulary, and book selection. A great book for all parents. **BRS; $12.95**

Expand Your Child's Vocabulary: A Twelve-Week Plan
by Carl B. Smith

A dozen super strategies for vocabulary growth—because word power is part of success at all stages of life. **BEYC; $7.95**

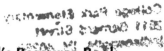

Elementary Grammar: A Child's Resource Book
by Carl B. Smith
A handy source of answers and explanations for young learners and their parents.
BG1; $13.95

Intermediate Grammar: A Student's Resource Book
by Carl B. Smith
A student's grammatical lifesaver! Complete explanations and examples, plus a handy punctuation guide. **BG2; $16.95**

Grammar Handbook for Home and School
by Carl B. Smith
A quick reference with concise explanations of the basics of English grammar and punctuation. The perfect companion to Intermediate Grammar. **BGH; $8.95**

❧ ❧ ❧

The Successful Learner Series

The Confident Learner: Help Your Child Succeed in School
by Marjorie R. Simic, Melinda McClain, and Michael Shermis
An easy-to-read guide for parents on raising a child who is ready and motivated to learn. Includes ways to work with your child's teacher and school. **BTCL; $9.95**

The Curious Learner: Help Your Child Develop Academic and Creative Skills
by Marjorie R. Simic, Melinda McClain, and Michael Shermis
Shows parents how to support their child's success in any subject by reinforcing school learning in the home. Parents learn to encourage their children's natural curiosity. **BCL; $9.95**

Order Information

To order copies of this book or the other resources listed above, please call or mail your order to

Family Literacy Center/EDINFO Press
Indiana University
P.O. Box 5953
Bloomington, IN 47407
Phone: 800-925-7853 • Fax: 812-331-2776

Please include 10% for shipping and handling, with a minimum of $3.00.